Producing for the Web

Producing for the Web is a clear and practical guide to the planning, setting up and management of a web site. It gives readers a comprehensive overview of the current technologies available for online communications and shows how to use them for maximum effect when designing a web site.

Producing for the Web sets out the practical toolkit that a web producer will require to create a site, from web and image editors to information processing and program applications. Supported by a regularly updated and comprehensive web site at **www.producing.routledge.com**, *Producing for the Web* includes:

- an introduction to the Internet and the world wide web
- illustrated examples of good page design and site content
- online support, tutorials and information on latest technologies at www.producing.routledge.com
- advice on content, maintenance and how to use sites effectively
- ideas on how to maximise available programs and applications
- tips on writing and style
- a discussion about ethics, copyright and regulation
- an extensive list of resources and Internet terminology.

Jason Whittaker is a lecturer in journalism, media and English at Falmouth College of Arts, where he specialises in web design and online journalism. He was previously editor of *PC Advisor* magazine.

Media Skills

SERIES EDITOR: RICHARD KEEBLE
CITY UNIVERSITY, LONDON
SERIES ADVISERS: WYNFORD HICKS AND JENNY MCKAY
NAPIER UNIVERSITY, SCOTLAND

The *Media Skills* series provides a concise and thorough introduction to a rapidly changing media landscape. Each book is written by media and journalism lecturers or experienced professionals and is a key resource for a particular industry. Offering helpful advice and information and using practical examples from print, broadcast and digital media, as well as discussing ethical and regulatory issues, *Media Skills* books are essential guides for students and media professionals.

Also in this series:

English for Journalists, 2nd edition
Wynford Hicks

Writing for Journalists
Wynford Hicks with Sally Adams and Harriett Gilbert

Interviewing for Radio
Jim Beaman

Find more details of current *Media Skills* books and forthcoming titles at **www.producing.routledge.com**

Producing for the Web

Jason Whittaker

LONDON AND NEW YORK

First published 2000
by Routledge
11 New Fetter Lane, London EC4P 4EE

Simultaneously published in the USA and Canada
by Routledge
29 West 35th Street, New York, NY 10001

Routledge is an imprint of the Taylor & Francis Group

Typeset in Goudy Old Style and Scala Sans by Taylor & Francis Books Ltd
Printed and bound in Great Britain by TJ International Ltd, Padstow, Cornwall

British Library Cataloguing in Publication Data
A catalogue record for this book is available from the British Library

Library of Congress Cataloging in Publication Data
Whittaker, Jason.
Producing for the Web / Jason Whittaker.
Includes bibliographical references and index.
1. Web sites. 2. Web publishing. I. Title.

TK5105.888. W48 2000
005.2'76–dc21   00–023759

ISBN 0–415–23113–2 (hb)
ISBN 0–415–23114–0 (pb)

Contents

Illustrations

Acknowledgements

I would like to thank my colleagues – fellow lecturers, students and especially the staff at *PC Advisor* – for support, comments and suggestions, and I would like to acknowledge the assistance provided by the Falmouth College of Arts Research Fund. Particular thanks are due to Sam, for permission to use her photographs, as well as to Adobe and Macromedia for providing software and useful information.

Introduction

WHAT THIS BOOK IS

This book is about producing web sites and using one of the most important parts of the Internet, the world wide web, to maximum effect. The web, which was established in the early 1990s and emerged as a mass medium in the second half of that decade, has attracted a huge amount of attention from the more traditional media as well as academic, business and, of course, computer-using communities.

The web holds out the promise of publishing and communication on a potentially global scale to anyone with access to a computer and online connection. Producing a web site can be pleasurable in itself, developing technical, writing and design skills that culminate in well-crafted pages. When computers work well (and they do not, it must be admitted, always work well), they enable people to develop ideas and achieve things that could previously only be done by experts.

At the same time, these skills – writing about interests and passions, creating graphics and laying out pages, programming scripts and interactive elements – are becoming more important than ever at the start of a new century. Web production and management is becoming a career for more and more people rather than a hobby. Web producers therefore need to understand the principles of how sites can work effectively and what abilities they need to develop for this new medium, both on a technical level and to communicate proficiently.

This book is a practical guide for anyone interested in the principles of web production, whether students, professionals or those who may be interested in developing their design skills for personal interests. Creating web sites is no longer the preserve of computer engineers, programmers and scientists but is open to a much wider group.

Part of the reason for the massive explosion of the web is that designing sites and taking part in this expanding, sprawling, often chaotic medium can be incredible fun. Consequently, although this book is aimed at professionals seeking to develop their skills in web production, it should also be read by those with a desire to expand their imagination into a new sphere.

WHAT THIS BOOK IS NOT

Although this book contains instructions for creating web sites, it is not a manual for particular applications. Most of the books published for use with the Internet and computers are generally aimed at learning a particular program or set of programming techniques. The aim of this book is different. The guides that are provided in the following chapters and on the accompanying web site are designed to be transferable across a number of applications, but are also provided as a basis for thinking about why such skills are necessary and how they are best used.

Nor is this a book about the web and the Internet. Although some background is given as to where the web has come from and why it is important, the main aim of such information is to provide a practical context for producing sites. You will not find instructions on using the Internet or computers in this book. The assumption is that you will already have some familiarity with using a browser and an operating system to save and open files.

This book does not offer reviews of web sites nor purport to be a guide to finding the best sites for particular tasks on the Internet. Examples of good practice and useful web addresses are included, particularly when they illustrate a certain technique or style, but a book of this type cannot, and should not, claim to be a comprehensive listing of an ever-changing medium.

By using this book, you will gain a grounding in the technologies and practical skills that are necessary to create a web site as well as an understanding of ways to plan and promote it to reach as many people as possible.

WHY PRODUCERS?

There are several terms used to describe workers involved in web-site production. Some of these are familiar from other media. There are, for example, writers and journalists who generate copy for a web site in the same fashion as staff writers for newspapers and magazines, as well as editors organising content, establishing production calendars and commissioning writers.

Other people may have links to other media but with slight differences. Web designers, for example, may share similarities with art directors and production staff on a magazine, while content-providers creating animation, audio and video for a site may possess some of the same skills as broadcasters for television and radio. In such cases, specialist knowledge of an application such as Quark XPress or Avid may be replaced by knowledge of Dreamweaver or Flash, but with the convergence of digital technology in more traditional forms of publishing and broadcasting there is considerable scope for crossover.

Finally, there are roles that appear to be more specific to the web, most notably that of web master which tends to cover technical and managerial skills. The role of web manager often applies to those members of a team who are responsible for meeting deadlines, allocating resources, managing staff and making strategic decisions about the content of a site, similar to the roles of editors, publishers, producers and directors in other media. In other cases, the web manager will also be responsible for the maintenance of a site, writing scripts, ensuring security and installing software, similar to a sound or video engineer; in other organisations these roles are devolved to a separate IT department.

This book uses the term producers to cover all of the above roles. There is, of course, the danger of confusion: if you are interested in web design to advance your career, for example, it is important to be aware that some companies and organisations will be looking for individuals to fulfil very specific roles. Nonetheless, as in other media web producers are frequently called upon to be multi-tasking. Just as a radio broadcaster may be his or her own sound technician, producer and editor, so web professionals may be called upon to provide different services at different times.

Finally, if you are looking to create a site for personal pleasure, there is a sense in which you are a writer, artist, editor, manager and publisher rolled into one, responsible not just for generating content but also for its distribution and maintenance. While one of the aims of this book is to enable students and professionals to specialise in their chosen field, the ability to direct and shape your own work to an almost unprecedented degree can be incredibly liberating. As one famous multimedia self-publisher, William Blake, remarked, 'I must Create a System, or be enslav'd by another Mans.'

HOW TO USE THIS BOOK

Obviously this book can be read by beginning at the beginning and continuing until you reach the end. Indeed, the chapters are arranged cumulatively, building on concepts, techniques and procedures introduced in previous sections. At the same time, the book is roughly divided into two halves: the first deals with important preparation work that is required to make a web site a success, while the second half deals much more with the mechanics of producing such a site.

In addition, chapters have been organised so that each section may serve as a reference or introduction to a particular aspect of web production. You may, for example, be looking for a particular image or web editor, want to know the difference between Java and ActiveX, or need to understand how to code a rollover button. Thus the book has also been designed to encourage readers to browse as required.

One of the problems with writing about the web (or, indeed, any aspect of computers) is that there is a huge quantity of technical terms. While much of this is jargon, some of it apparently employed for no other reason than to confuse the novice, much is also precise and to attempt to describe it in 'plain English' can result in sentences that are extremely convoluted. For example, HTML, one of the more common terms, is a useful acronym once the principles of hypertext markup language have been explained. I have tried to avoid using technical language simply for its own sake, but where a technical term is first introduced it is highlighted in bold.

Likewise, there are plenty of 'recipes' in the book for creating web pages that require the reader to enter very specific information. When the text indicates that you must type in the text as it appears on the page, a mono-spaced font is used, such as `<TITLE>Hello World</TITLE>`. The reason for this convention is that using quotation marks can be confusing: such punctuation marks are frequently employed in programming code for a specific purpose. Another convention is that web addresses are written without the prefix http:// (which is inserted by most modern browsers in any case). Thus, for example, the address for the popular search engine Excite is denoted www.excite.com.

Because the web is such a rapidly evolving medium, there may be some discrepancies between certain sites and what is printed in each chapter. I have attempted to use sites that seem to be the most stable as examples of different techniques and approaches, but sometimes the most interesting work is that produced by individuals who may not be able to sustain a site. Likewise, while writing this book, one of the main web editor packages, Dreamweaver, was re-released as a new version. The book deals with the most up-to-date information at the time of publication, but it is also designed to be used with the companion web site at www.producing.routledge.com: this site contains updates about software and news that will be of interest to web producers (see 'The *Producing for the Web* site' on page 6).

WHAT YOU NEED

The most obvious requirement to use this book is access to a computer and an Internet connection. While you do not actually need to upload files to a site, an Internet connection is useful both for downloading files from the web and accessing sites that will be useful for web production.

Web design can be incredibly simple in terms of computing power. At a time when computers double in power every eighteen months or so, the web is often limited by the much slower bottleneck caused by the connection to the Internet. Some of the best web design therefore follows the principle that less is more, and it is possible to construct many sites with little more than a text editor such as NotePad on the PC or SimpleText on the Mac.

That said, it is realistic to use a computer that has enough power to run a decent editor and a graphics application to edit images at the very least. This does not need to be the latest Intel or Motorola chip – an older Pentium or Mac will often be more than sufficient for web design, which should *not* consist of manipulating large files.

No assumption has been made about your knowledge of web production, and this book begins with the most basic aspects of web design before proceeding to more complex features. However, there are some things that this book does not cover. It is assumed, for example, that you are familiar with the operating system on the computer you use, that you can open and save files and know how to navigate through the folders on your hard disk. Likewise, this book does not include instructions on how to use browsers to find sites or how to connect to an Internet

Service Provider. It is assumed that you are an Internet user who wishes to move to the next stage and produce your own sites.

THE *PRODUCING FOR THE WEB* SITE

Because of the nature of this particular book, the companion web site at www.producing.routledge.com/default.htm is extremely important. You can use this book without referring to it (for example, using your own images and texts instead of those downloaded from the site), but the site is an expansion of this book.

Although the site does not contain information on issues concerning planning and maintenance that are important to someone planning a professional career in web production, it does expand on the tutorials given in this book for different applications and technologies. As information about the web and web production can change very rapidly, it also includes updates about the latest developments.

The site is arranged into the following main areas:

- **Production news:** This includes the latest information relevant to web producers, such as updates to browsers and software, new releases and changes to Internet specifications. The news can be accessed at www.producing.routledge.com/news.htm.

- **Production techniques:** These are extended tutorials for specific packages rather than introductions to principles of web design as in this book. It is assumed that you will have read chapters four and five in particular to understand why these techniques are used before accessing the tutorials at www.producing.routledge.com/techniques.htm to see how they are implemented by different programs.

- **Production resources:** Here is an extended and annotated list of resources listed before the index in this book, as well as files to create the sample site outlined in this book at www.producing.routledge.com/resources.htm.

- **Sample site:** Chapters four and five outline different web production processes with reference to a sample site that you will build using the resources accessed at the above address. To view the sample site, go to www.producing.routledge.com/kernow/default.htm.

1
World-wide information and communication

The reasons for producing a web site are numerous: it may be part of a project assignment for a university or college course or a marketing strategy for your business; you may have a personal interest that you wish to publish to a wider audience, or you need to set up a site to promote the activities of a group to which you belong. Whatever the reason for creating a web site, whether as part of a programme of study or the development of career skills, web production and publishing are attracting a great deal of attention from employers, the media and the general public as exciting and important new ventures. What was, less than a decade ago, the preserve of enthusiasts has become a mass medium to compare with television, radio and print.

This chapter will introduce the background of the **Internet**, what it is and how it works. As the aim of this book is to provide advice for those seeking to develop their practical skills, some of the theoretical concerns relating to the Internet such as its history have been kept fairly short. It is not a technical introduction, though it will also introduce some of the jargon associated with the Internet and web: it is possible to create a web site with a minimum of technical knowledge as to how the Internet actually operates. Nonetheless, some technical knowledge (such as why servers are required to deliver pages) can improve your skills as a web producer.

Another aim of this chapter is to discuss some of the wider concerns affecting the Net, particularly those relating to legislation that may affect designers, producers and content-providers. The international nature of the web, which was built into the Internet almost from the ground up, has had important implications for the way that information is transmitted around the world, and may also affect other areas, such as the way we conduct trade and commerce, in the future.

THE INTERNET AND THE WEB

What is the Internet?

The Internet is attracting more and more attention as the next step for world-wide computing. The term, Internet, refers to the connection of millions of computers and users – from 147 million users in February 1999 (up from 61 million in 1996) to an estimated 300 million in 2000 and 720 million by 2005 according to the *Computer Industry Almanac*, 1999 – across the whole world with the potential for many more.

The common starting point for any definition of the Internet is as a 'network of networks'. The Internet is a Wide Area Network (**WAN**), millions of PCs, Apple Macs, mainframes, laptops and other computers joined by cables, satellites and radio waves across the globe. When most people think of the Internet, the first thing that springs into their minds is the hardware, the physical links connecting these diverse parts. Actually, the Internet is equally a collection of communication **protocols**, rules governing the transfer of information such as TCP/IP (Transfer Control Protocol/Internet Protocol), that allows very different types of computers to communicate with each other. It is this series of protocols, outlasting advances in hardware, that is the lifeblood of the Net.

People tend to think of the web and the Internet as the same entity. In fact, the web developed in the 1990s as a means of exchanging documents that piggy-backed across the infrastructure of hardware and software that had developed by that time. The Internet is the larger collection of network services (including email and file transfer), most of which have been integrated into web browsers.

A brief history of the Internet

The beginning of the Internet is conventionally dated to the late 1960s, though one convenient starting point is the launch of Sputnik in 1957, the first artificial satellite that began the space race and the global telecommunications system that the Internet would plug into.

Following the launch of Sputnik, the Advanced Research Projects Agency (ARPA) was founded, essentially funded by the US Department of Defense but also oriented towards academic research. As John Naughton points out in his book *A Brief History of the Future* (1999), the actual development of the network of networks we use today owed more to simple academic and financial concerns of using computers more efficiently by networking them together, but the cold war remained an important impetus to the development of ARPA.

Between 1963 and 1967, ARPA investigated the feasibility of building such a network and selected nineteen participants to join in **ARPANET**, as it had become known, work beginning in 1968–9. Much of the essential work at ARPA consisted of providing the protocols that would enable the physical backbone to communicate. Of especial importance was **packet** switching software: rather than sending information as a single file, it is split into small packets, each of which can be sent via different hosts so that significant amounts of the file reach its destination even in the event of a particular host being unavailable.

International connections were established in 1973 with the University College of London and the Royal Radar Establishment in Norway. Work also proceeded on improving the protocols that remain the standard for Internet transmissions such as File Transfer Protocol (**FTP**) and Transfer Control Protocol (**TCP**). In 1979, the US National Science Foundation (**NSF**) established a computer science research network.

More significant development began in the 1980s, and it is hardly a coincidence that the largest computer network in the world began to take off as the personal computer gained ground, introducing more and more people to the notion of computing. The 1980s also saw the introduction of Domain Name Services (**DNS**), to allocate addresses to host computers. Throughout the late 1980s, with DNS in place, all these different networks could access computers anywhere across the network, meaning that the Internet was fully established by 1990, the year when ARPANET, its work finished, ceased to exist. The next decade was to establish the Internet as a wider communication medium with the spread of email and development of the web.

At the European Centre for Nuclear Research (CERN), a consultant, Tim Berners-Lee, had written a short program entitled modestly 'Enquire-Within-Upon-Everything', linking documents. ENQUIRE, as it came to be known, was Berners-Lee's big idea: it became even bigger in 1989, when he submitted a paper entitled 'Information Management: A Proposal'. In 1990, the first text web browser was developed at CERN and so the world wide web was born.

CERN continued to develop the web as an academic tool, but by the end of 1992 only 26 hosts were serving web sites, and even in early 1994 there were only 1,500 registered web servers. The boom in web – and Internet –

growth shown in Figure 1.1 came with the development of Mosaic, a graphical browser capable of displaying images as well as text, by Marc Andreessen at the National Center for Supercomputing Applications.

In 1994, Andreessen left to form Mosaic Communications, the precursor to Netscape. What was most significant about Andreessen's work was that he actively began to promote the Internet as a platform, like **UNIX**, or Windows. Nineteen ninety-five was the year of the web: Netscape Navigator had an estimated ten million users world wide and, when the company went public, Netscape Communications was valued at over $2.5 billion on Wall Street.

By this time, Microsoft had 80 per cent of the operating system market, making founder Bill Gates the richest man in the world. Microsoft initially dismissed the Internet as a fad, intending to supplant it with its own Microsoft Network (MSN), but by late 1995 Gates had turned the company around when it was clear that MSN would do no such thing. That the most powerful software company in the world should wish to stake the future of its success on the web is an indication of just how important it has become.

Internet structure

The Internet backbone comprises two main parts: the hardware/communications network, and the protocols governing data transfer across that network. The actual computer hardware is relatively insignificant, in that it can be upgraded regularly and is changed frequently. More important is the communications infrastructure, the cables and satellite links, which are much more difficult to change and limit the **bandwidth**, the amount of data, that can be transferred from computer to computer. A common metaphor for bandwidth is a pipe, but this is incredibly misleading: the assumption is that if you increase the width of the pipe, you can pour more data down it. A better metaphor is of a road network: simply widening roads may not help traffic jams, but smaller and faster cars, as well as improved traffic control systems, may help more drivers get from A to B.

Protocols control how data is transferred across that infrastructure, the most important ones being collected together as TCP/IP (Transfer Control Protocol/Internet Protocol). TCP/IP operates on four levels: network access (to facilitate transmission and routing of packets); network protocols (governing the delivery service); transfer protocols (ensuring the machines are capable of receiving and sending packets);

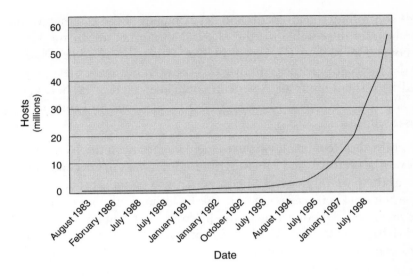

Figure 1.1 **Internet growth**

Source: Internet Software Consortium, www.isc.com

and application protocols (either applications themselves, or providing service to applications running across the Internet).

IP addressing is the basic means by which computers are identified on the Net. This is a 32-bit number that uniquely identifies each host and network as four octets from 0 to 255 (for example 10.126.58.192). Along with the IP address is a host name, a more easily memorised name (such as www.ibm.com): the domain name service (DNS) is a table holding lists of hosts, so that when a user sends an email, requests are passed up the Internet chain until eventually they find a DNS table listing that host. Information passed from computers is broken into packets, each one with a heading that identifies that packet: when they reach their destination, the packets are reassembled into the complete message. Some of the protocols governing TCP/IP are error-checking protocols: if the message is incomplete, the destination computer requests the packet to be sent again.

Internet administration

Who owns the Internet? Although a common perception of the Internet is that it is an anarchic place, there are in fact several bureaucratic levels controlling the protocols and development of the Internet as well as companies responsible for the physical infrastructure. In the UK, a few companies such as BT, Pipex, EUNet, CompuServe and AOL control the Internet pipelines entering this country. But even they are provided by a small group of American companies such as AT&T, Cable and Wireless and Sprint, who own transatlantic cables and communications satellites.

Yet, whilst these companies are extremely important to the Net, they do not own the protocols and data which are as important to telecommunications as the physical network. The Internet was previously administered by the National Science Foundation (NSF); although this is no longer the case, any network connecting to the Internet has to submit to standards ratified by the Internet Architecture Board (**IAB**, www.iab.org). This board oversees technical support and reporting committees designed to maintain the protocols for communicating across the Net.

The IAB and other organisations can be useful to a web producer, particularly ones such as the World Wide Web Consortium (**W3C**, www.w3c.org), which provides information on the development of new web protocols. Essentially, these offer archives of information that can help producers determine the future development of the web. Most of these bodies have their roots in academic and scientific research; their work has been important because the Net is a prime example of an open architecture, applying standards that enable different technologies to work together.

The principal non-profit organisations involved with technical administration on the web include the **IETF** (Internet Engineering Task Force, www.ietf.org) and **ISOC** (Internet Society, www.isoc.org) that monitor general Internet standards, and **ICANN** (Internet Corporation for Assigned Names and Numbers, www.icann.org), which handles domain name registration and IP address allocation.

Setting standards

The process of implementing technical standards across the Internet requires a quality-control procedure involving some or all of the above groups. While it is uncommon for a web producer to seek to implement a new standard across the Net, some understanding of the procedure can be useful for those who wish to keep up with new developments on the Internet such as XML.

The 'standards track' system begins with an **RFC** (Request for Comments), and progresses through the following stages before becoming an Internet standard: the RFC is circulated to an Internet Engineering Task Force working group and, if accepted, becomes an Internet Draft that is further discussed by the IETF. Technical discussion now takes as long as necessary to iron out problems (typically six months or longer), whereupon it may become a Proposed Standard. If it is accepted by the Internet Engineering Steering Group (IESG, www.ietf.org/iesc.html), then it becomes a Draft Standard, and waits another minimum six months before possibly being accepted as an Internet Standard. During this time it can be discussed by members of other organisations such as the W3C.

This lengthy process has been used to iron out incompatibilities in the fundamental architecture of the Internet such as FTP, **HTTP** and TCP/IP, as well as other developments such as Internet Printing and IP routing for mobile hosts. While the process of developing standards is rather arcane from the standpoint of most web producers, Requests for Comments can be a useful tool for determining the future shape of the Internet.

HOW THE INTERNET WORKS

The basic architecture of the Internet is what is known as a **client-server** model. A server, a computer running special software, hosts a range of services such as email and web pages which are accessed by client software running on a remote computer. Most users access servers via a dial-up account with an Internet Service Provider (**ISP**); chapter two covers some of the details web producers may need to take into account when selecting an ISP, but it is worth knowing some basic details about how ISPs connect their users to the Net.

An ISP is a company or organisation that provides dial-up accounts by purchasing a leased line connection and then dividing its use between subscribers. There are hundreds in the UK and thousands world wide. Dial-up ISPs offer Point-to-Point Protocol (**PPP**) or Serial Line Internet Protocol (**SLIP**) accounts users, the superior PPP accounts being most common.

PPP communications programs, such as Windows Dial-Up Networking, connect to the network by dialling via a **modem**, then log into the network with a user name and password. Windows application producers created a standard way for Internet clients to communicate called Winsock (short for Windows sockets, the protocols governing the ports listed under 'Servers, clients and ports' below) and Dial-Up Networking is Winsock compatible. The equivalent standard for Macs is called Open Transport/PPP in earlier versions of the MacOs, Apple Remote Access in the latest version.

Protocols and services

After connecting to the Internet, there are various different protocols and services used to transmit information to the client.

Web documents The web is a collection of sites, or documents, which share a specialised protocol, Hypertext Transfer Protocol (HTTP), enabling different operating systems to share the same data. Web documents are formatted in **HTML**, or Hypertext Markup Language, to standardise the presentation of text, graphics and links to other sites, with the end result that a document will look more or less the same in a browser for Windows, MacOS or UNIX. Clicking on a **hypertext** link, which is an embedded address or **URL**, will effect a transfer of information, whether to another document, image or file. Hypertext is something of a misnomer, as links within a web document can also be anchored to images.

HTTP Hypertext Transfer Protocol enables the easy retrieval of documents from the Internet regardless of where they are held. HTTP defines URLs not only for the web but also for FTP and Usenet sites, making it an extremely useful means of accessing a wide range of documents. To implement data transfer as simply as possible, HTTP provides web authors with the ability to embed hypertext links within documents.

URL A Uniform Resource Locator (usually signified as http://) is an address identifying an Internet document's type and location. URLs are absolute or relative, the former indicating precisely where a document is to be found on the web, the latter assuming that the file is a document somewhere on the same site.

FTP As a network of networks, the Internet is a large repository of software and information. Before the web boom, an older method of accessing this data was via the extremely useful method of FTP

(File Transfer Protocol), which has subsequently been absorbed into many browsers. FTP was developed to enable users to run client programs and access remote archives managed by FTP servers. Using a web browser FTP sites are accessed by following links, while FTP client software requires users to log on to a site.

Usenet   Usenet consists of several thousand newsgroups on a vast number of topics, newsgroups being identified by prefixes such as rec. (recreational) or alt. (alternative). Accessing Usenet enables users to read articles of post replies for other subscribers and most web browsers are capable of reading Usenet news. There are few or no formal rules governing Usenet forums (but plenty of informal ones), and this can make Usenet overwhelming at first. If you have a special interest, however, a newsgroup may be a cheap and convenient means of retrieving information.

IRC   Internet Relay Chat is the Internet's real-time facility, enabling users to log on to the Net at the same time and carry on sentence-by-sentence conversations. IRC runs via channels, discussion areas which exist in their thousands; you can send messages to everyone on such a channel, or to individuals.

Telnet   Telnet is a protocol allowing users to log into a remote computer and use it as their own. The most common uses for Telnet are logging into a computer to pick up email or to use specific programs. When a PC is connected to a remote computer, it acts very much like a terminal, with Telnet protocol emulating terminal standards which used to govern connection to the large mainframes.

Servers, clients and ports

While many Internet users can use the web with minimum knowledge of how its computers are connected as a network, web producers, especially those responsible for managing sites, may find a basic understanding helpful, particularly when loading sites onto remote computers. The above protocols and services require the following servers:

Mail servers   Handling incoming and outgoing mail, Post Office Protocol (POP, or **POP3**) servers store incoming mail and

Simple Mail Transfer Protocol (**SMTP**) servers send outgoing mail.

Web servers These hold web pages that are downloaded to client browsers.

FTP servers These store files that can be transferred (via the file transfer protocol) to and from a computer with a suitable client.

News servers News servers hold text messages – Usenet newsgroup articles – which are a popular forum for discussion on the Internet.

IRC servers These are switchboards for Internet Relay Chat, real-time based communication online.

A single computer can host more than one server, so that small ISPs will tend to have one computer running a mail server, web server and newsgroup server. To handle requests from different clients, each server type responds to information sent to a specific **port**, the input for that specific Internet service. Port numbers are increasingly handled by client software, but occasionally it may be necessary to specify the port when connecting to an ISP for the first time, for example to upload files via FTP onto a remote server (see Table 1.1).

For example, in some cases connecting to an FTP server would require you to enter the address followed by a colon and port number ftp://ftp.myaddress.com:21.

Browsers

Browsers are, strictly speaking, programs designed to communicate with web servers on the Internet, but common usage extends the term for the two most popular browsers, Netscape Communicator (incorporating

Table 1.1   Server ports

Port number	Service
21	FTP
23	Telnet
25	SMTP
80	Web
110	POP3

Navigator) and Microsoft Internet Explorer, to cover email, newsgroup and other functions. These browsers also use **plug-ins**, applications loaded by the browser to extend its functionality, to perform certain tasks such as playing certain audio-visual files or displaying some 3-D sites.

A web browser utilises HTTP to communicate with a server and then translates HTML code to display pages on the client computer. At its absolute minimum, this means a browser must display text, but since the incorporation of images users have come to expect much more, and the latest versions of Navigator and Internet Explorer (IE) can display video, sound, 3-D and interactive animation. The versatility of browsers has made them increasingly important outside the web, so that from IE 4 and Windows 98 onwards, Microsoft has begun to build its browser into the operating system to display files and images.

Competition between Netscape and Microsoft is fierce, and was the main contributor to the anti-trust case against Microsoft in 1999. While this has had many negative effects, principally issues relating to compatibility, it has also helped to fuel development of web technologies as computing power has increased since the early 1990s. Both companies tend to update their browsers on a regular basis, these being available from their websites:

home.netscape.com/download

www.microsoft.com/ie

These are not the only browsers available on the web: Opera (www.operasoftware.com) is a recent newcomer and visitors with older machines may still be using Mosaic, the first graphical browser, and Lynx, a text-only browser. Most browsers have the same basic layout – a menu bar, toolbars (with back, forward, reload and other buttons located here), an address or location window, the main viewing window where pages are displayed, and a status bar indicating such things as download time as in Figure 1.2.

Passwords and security

Internet security is a hot topic for any user of the Net, but never more so than for the web producer who will be involved in administering a site: while there are various flaws in operating systems such as Windows NT that have been routinely picked up by hackers, it still remains the case that cracking passwords remains the easiest way to break into a web site.

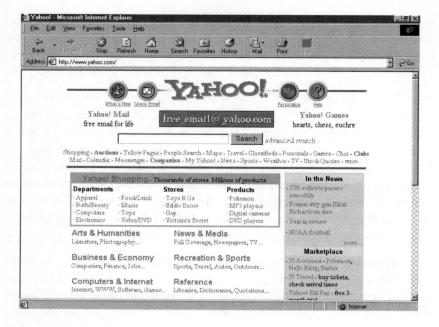

Figure 1.2   **Yahoo! displayed in the browser Internet Explorer 5**

We will be covering issues around security in more detail later in this book, but as an Internet and email account has to have a password, it is worth establishing some proper procedures as early as possible.

A good password should be easy to remember but hard to guess. A combination of random numbers, letters and cases such as pB6I9dsO is likely to keep out everyone – including you – while keeping a note of passwords anywhere is the simplest way for them to be discovered and abused.

TIPS FOR USING PASSWORDS

- **Don't use the same password for everything:** A password for reading an online journal or newspaper could be much more troublesome if it's the same one you use to access online web space. Likewise, anything that requires saving your credit card number on file requires a very strong password.

- **Don't use English words or names:** While passwords are usually encrypted, a typical way to try and crack them is simply to run through a large number of words.

> * **Try acronyms and include numbers:** A common technique for passwords is to combine acronyms of names and numbers, such as 'wadsorps99' (your password for 1999).
>
> * **Don't write down a password:** If you have to keep a record of your password, write down a hint to it instead.

THE INTERNET AND REGULATION

Privacy, security and the law

With the monumental growth of the Internet over the past five years, the rapid spread of international communication via email and the web has brought its own problems and dilemmas for web producers, users and regulators.

In the UK, for example, the first draft of the Electronic Communications Bill was drafted to help build confidence in e-commerce and its underlying technology. Like the 1996 US Telecommunications Bill, this rather uncontroversial aim was overtaken by media interest in one section of such legislation. In 1996, it was the attempt by Congress to regulate online decency via the Communications Decency Act (CDA); in 1999 the attempt by the UK government to 'maintain the effectiveness of existing law enforcement powers in the face of increasing criminal use of encryption' (Draft Electronic Communications Bill: Draft Regulatory Impact Assessment, July 1999). The right for police and other enforcement agencies to seize encryption keys has since been moved to a Regulation of Investigatory Powers Bill.

The question of the regulation of privacy and security across the Internet, whether by governments or by other organisations, is one with civil and legal implications that will affect a wide range of Internet users, but what changes most affect web producers?

Copyright

As Nicholas Negroponte pointed out in his 1995 book *Being Digital*, most people in the early 1990s had not recognised the potential of the computer and Internet for making perfect copies of information, whether text, images, audio or video. What was more, the ability to copy such data and transmit it around the world was open to anyone with a computer and modem. Previous international legislation had always approached copyright from the standpoint that significant infractions would be centralised in some way, and that copying via media such as video or audio tape would always involve some deterioration of the original source material.

Concerns over copyright, however, prompted the European Parliament to propose the Copyright in the Information Society Bill early in 1999. The aim of this bill was to enforce copyright regulations, taking into account the ease with which data can now be copied. When the bill was first announced, it caused considerable consternation amongst ISPs because it excluded all copying, including temporary Internet **caches**, as part of the effort to protect copyright holders from Internet-based piracy.

As the European Internet Service Providers Association (EuroISPA) lobbied for amendments, the bill was not passed in this form. While copyright is an issue for many service providers, the most immediate problem with this bill was that it was seen as implementing decisions without conferring with the industry, with the potential risk of losing a competitive edge in Europe.

Spam

While copyright infringement has tended to concern producers and governments more than users, the problem of junk mail, or **spam**, is one appreciated by just about everyone. Spamming occurs when an individual or company sends out a message (often anonymously) to a list of recipients. Such messages may be illegal or unsuitable for the recipient, such as pornographic links or fraudulent get-rich-quick schemes; even if this is not the case, spam is usually paid for by the person downloading the message and can be a major irritation, with accounts becoming unusable because of the large number of unsolicited emails.

The problems of spamming have even caused some ISPs, such as Virgin in the UK, to sue their own customers because spammers who send out hundreds of thousands of emails may cause the ISP's mail server to be placed on the Realtime Blackhole List, a list circulated among major ISPs that identifies domain names originating large numbers of unsolicited emails.

The 1998 Data Protection Act was criticised for its failure to address the problem of spam, emphasising as it did the responsibility of users for their own data. There are proposals before the UK and EC governments to address this issue, but the individual is not entirely helpless in the face of spamming. Rather than simply deleting a message or replying to it, users can often work out where an email came from and complain to the ISP that delivered it.

Obscenity

Two other major concerns for Internet users and regulators have been obscenity and defamation. In 1996, the US government attempted to control the publication of obscene material on the Internet by means of the Communications Decency Act, part of a wider telecommunications bill. This proved to be a rather draconian and heavy-handed regulatory tool in that the letter of the law applied more excessive regulation against the web than against any other medium, with the act being declared unconstitutional within months. In the UK, the 1990 Computer Misuse Act has been used to deal with online obscenity amongst other things.

As with libel, the relatively small number of cases brought against publishers of obscene material has led many to assume that the Net cannot be regulated, but this is not the case. In the case of *Regina* v. *Waddon* in 1999, for example, Graham Waddon was charged with publishing obscene images on the Internet according to the provisions of the 1959 Obscene Publications Act (OPA). Under this act, it is illegal to publish obscene material with a view to commercial gain, with punishment consisting of up to three years' imprisonment, an unlimited fine or both.

The fact that a large amount of pornography on the web is free makes it difficult to apply the OPA, but Waddon was charging visitors to view his material, although his defence was that these files were housed on a server in another country. An amendment in the 1994 Criminal Justice and Public Order Act, however, has clarified publication to include transmission of material, so that Waddon was found guilty of electronic transmission of such files to a server, meaning that a person could be found guilty of breaking the law in the UK even if the ISP was in a different country.

Libel

The lack of prosecutions or settlements for libel, like obscenity, has been taken to reflect the *laissez-faire* nature of the web. Nonetheless, cases in the United States have been influential, particularly in determining the role of the ISP.

Two cases, *Cubby* v. *CompuServe* (1991) and *Oakmont* v. *Prodigy* (1995), provided apparently contradictory evidence as to the state of ISPs, whether they are publishers of material or free carriers (rather like telephone companies). In the case of CompuServe, the court acknowledged the instantaneous nature of Internet postings and that it was not feasible for the ISP to examine every message. Exactly the opposite point was made in the Prodigy case, but this was due to the fact that Prodigy, a family-oriented service, specifically claimed to regulate the contents of its bulletin boards. An ironic consequence, in the US at least, is that ISPs increasingly do not regulate bulletin-board postings at all to avoid being liable as publishers.

In the UK, the 1996 Defamation Act attempted to clarify the position of ISPs as secondary carriers, whereby if the ISP can demonstrate that due care is taken to monitor content, it is not liable, a so-called 'Section 1' defence. This can also be employed in line with other defences by a publisher, such as fair comment, justification and privilege. Rather than encourage a hands-off approach, the act attempts to encourage ISPs to monitor postings while accepting the impossibility of checking them all.

An interpretation of this act that appeared to protect ISPs, however, was thrown into doubt with the court case brought by Dr Laurence Godfrey against Demon in 1999, where it was held immaterial that Dr Godfrey was not a Demon customer, and that the material had not been posted by a Demon customer (it was a Usenet posting), but that the key point was Demon's refusal to remove the posting once Dr Godfrey had complained to the ISP about it. The case was also complicated by the fact that the posting was anonymous, meaning the plaintiff could not pursue the author.

While this particular case affected an ISP, libel is also an issue for web publishers, more so in that the defence of being a free carrier is not open to them. In many cases, web publishing can follow straightforward defamation rules for print and other media, but where a bulletin board, for example, is included on a web site, it is the producer's responsibility to manage this as much as is possible, meaning that postings must be monitored and, more importantly, a complaint-handling procedure should be in place. Should a complaint be received, access to the offending message should be *suspended* (the message does not need to be deleted) until it is assessed and a response made to the complainant ideally within twenty-four hours. It is also advisable to make clear limits of acceptable behaviour on a web site, particularly as to what material will be removed.

E-commerce

Many of the potential conflicts that will affect web producers revolve around e-commerce. The World Trade Organisation estimates that transactions across the Internet will account for some $300 billion in 2001, but the growth of e-commerce has so far outstripped its regulation. Many argue that such transactions should be largely unregulated if e-commerce is to develop, but if the Internet is seen as a primary site for fraud and poor services, this could be as effective in preventing the development of markets as restrictive laws.

Difficulties in regulation arise from the international nature of the Internet. For example, the 1974 Consumer Credit Act, which states that the credit card company assumes the responsibilities of the supplier for items valued over £100 which are not received or are faulty, only applies to transactions in the UK. Likewise, EU Directives on Data Protection and Telecommunication (implemented in the UK as the 1998 Data Protection Act) encourage Internet suppliers to provide protection for privacy, but again their remit is limited to the EU.

In practice in the UK, regulation covering electronic commerce has largely been implemented in the same fashion as for other forms of conducting business. In an incident that proved embarrassing for Argos in September 1999, the company's web site wrongly listed TVs at £2.99 instead of £299, resulting in hundreds of orders for these bargain items. Despite the fact that the only disclaimer was that items were 'subject to availability', Argos refused to honour these orders.

There is a common assumption that a supplier is legally obliged to sell an item at a stated price. In fact, displaying a price is merely an 'invitation to treat', and the supplier must agree to provide goods before a contract is established. In this case, therefore, Argos was legally entitled to refuse the offer made by potential customers.

However, although a contract is not formed until the supplier agrees to the offer made by a customer, there is a grey area around automated systems that accept credit cards or other forms of online payment; it may be that this constitutes acceptance on the part of the retailer, in which case there would be a binding contract. At the time of writing, there has not been litigation to clarify this matter, but developers thinking of setting up an e-commerce site should ensure that there are systems in place to check all transactions before fully automating the process.

2
Pre-production

Five years ago, the question 'Why the web?' had a very simple answer: because it was there. Now it is no longer enough for this medium to be cool simply because it represents new technology, it must also offer core benefits to users. As well as being useful for browsing the online history of *The Blair Witch Project*, the Internet – and the web especially – is becoming much more of a practical tool for commerce, entertainment and communication.

With the web, you can receive constantly changing reports on weather and travel, book tickets, locate and study for courses and receive information, goods and services in all areas from upgrading your computer to ordering groceries. Internet shopping is finally beginning to take off, with businesses moving beyond using the web simply for email and tele-working to providing online catalogues and credit services.

To utilise the benefits of the web requires careful pre-planning: before launching into web production, it is important to think strategically about the potential benefits that a web site may offer, how designers and users will connect to such a site and how projects will be maintained and developed.

FIRST STEPS

Why a web site?

The first questions to ask when considering the possibilities of a web site are: do you need it, and what can Internet communication achieve that traditional forms cannot?

With regard to the second question, the most obvious factor is the use of the Internet for communication via email and web pages. Like the telephone or fax, the Internet is (usually) fast but, like a letter, can be viewed or responded to at the user's convenience. It may not be as useful as the phone for reaching a quick decision between two people, but, because an email can consist of anything from a simple text message to a full blown multimedia file, it is a more versatile medium than any other.

Turning to whether a web site is necessary for a business or an individual such as a student looking to complete a project, an important consideration is whether the web will enhance or decrease productivity. The rationale for a web site can be summarised by the following questions:

- **What is it for and who is the intended audience?** Web sites can be used for many purposes, including sharing an interest, e-commerce, publicising goods and services, product branding, or public information services. Establishing the target audience is important as an indicator for whether the site will meet its aims: creating an information site for people without access to the web, for example, is not likely to achieve any significant objectives.

- **Can you afford a web site?** As well as the obvious category of hiring web space on a server (the cost of which which will almost certainly be negligible assuming the site is to be hosted on an ISP) and designing the site in the first place, this covers the expense of time as well as money to produce and maintain a web site. Even for larger companies there is the problem of ensuring sufficient time to update information and deal with the communications that (you hope) will be generated by the site.

- **What are your strategic aims?** You should decide what you are using the web site for, which could include assessing the demographics of customers or the current market place, or, if you are a student, whether producing a web site will fulfil your aims better than, say, an essay.

- **How will you judge the success of your site?** This includes setting in place criteria by which you can evaluate whether or not a site achieves your aims. For example, this may consist of basic statistical information such as the number of hits your site generates, or something more substantial, such as diverting phone calls from support lines to a web site or achieving pass grades for a student.

- **How will you promote your site?** If you are going to use the web seriously, don't complain if you forget to tell anyone and then receive a lacklustre response. Promotion can be as simple as including a URL on a business card, or as expensive as taking out advertising banners on other sites. One necessity is to register your site with search engines so that casual users will be able to find relevant information.

Internet or intranet?

For the aspiring web producer, probably the most important decision is whether you will be building an Internet or **intranet** web site. Both employ many of the same features and technologies (web pages linked to a server, often hosting some form of database) and the skills outlined in this book will, in most cases, apply to either, but the function of an intranet as opposed to an Internet site is often very different.

While an Internet site is built from the word go to be accessible to users with browsers on the world wide web, intranet sites may be housed entirely within a single geographical location. It is more likely, because they use protocols such as HTTP and FTP to transmit information, that intranets will be a hybrid, accessed by users within a company or at home and on the road, but with greater attention to security.

Although web sites and intranets share the same technologies, the requirements of their users are very different. Simply setting up a web server such as **Apache** or Microsoft **IIS** on a server in a company with some pages and a database does not constitute an intranet. An intranet that is not used by people will be a failure, so whereas a web site may be a success simply because it provides a link between your enthusiasms and the outside world, an intranet must have content that is compelling to its users.

To be fully successful, then, an intranet should invite its users to take ownership of that content. Most of the data within an organisation is not going to be controlled by one person (the web producer), so there should be the possibility of updating information by other people. This raises the spectre of security, particularly if users will access the site across the Internet, so designing an intranet requires additional attention to areas on a server where users will be able to add information and to those which are not to be accessed.

WORTH WHILE WEB

From its beginnings as an academic and research tool, the Internet has grown into a service for commerce and entertainment. Amongst the hardy stalwarts from the mid-1990s are Hotwired (www.hotwired.com) and the Time-Warner web site, Pathfinder (www.pathfinder.com).

As well as producing entertainment and news, there are plenty of sites that do what the web does best, providing information. Notable examples are Encyclopaedia Britannica (www.britannica.com) or Allexperts.com (www.allexperts.com), which puts you in touch with volunteers answering questions on different topics. In terms of establishing a presence, Amazon is obviously one of the biggest brand names, but British-based QXL.com (www.qxl.com) and Freeserve (www.freeserve.co.uk) have done their bit to show that innovation can take place outside the US.

Nor do web-ready entrepreneurs require millions to succeed. In the UK, Gameplay, one of the largest gaming businesses in the country, began life with £2,500 funding from the Prince's Trust, and has grown from a mail-order company to one that conducts business extensively across the web, with an annual turnover of £8m.

Figure 2.1   **Amazon.com is one of the most widely recognised web sites in the world**

CONNECTING TO THE WEB

Choosing an ISP

The first step for anyone involved in web production is obtaining an Internet connection. For students, Internet connections will probably be provided by the college or university; private users will need the services of an Internet Service Provider (ISP).

One of the biggest changes to ISPs since the end of the 1990s has been the widespread adoption of free services, following the rapid success of Dixon's FreeServe (www.freeserve.co.uk). It is, however, worth bearing in mind that some services such as ClaraNet (www.clara.net) offer cheaper or even free phone calls, so that using the Net for extended periods during peak time each month could actually save more money. British Telecom charges a dial-up fee that it shares with some services which either keep the money or, as with ClaraNet, pass part of it on as savings to the customer.

Something that is not offered in the free market, but is available from certain subscription ISPs, is co-hosting, whereby the ISP houses the web server: it remains the owner's machine, enabling them to run any **scripts** they require, but also provides a high bandwidth connection. In addition, companies such as Demon (www.demon.net) offer fixed ISP addresses, useful for businesses with their own server or network at the end of a leased line. For a summary of such services, see Table 2.1.

Table 2.1   Types of service

Service	Pros	Cons
Free ISP	Cheap to use; most now also provide web space	Unlikely to allow scripting; some servers slow because of high use
Subscription ISP	Offer wider range of services, such as support for scripting, particularly to businesses	Need to shop around: some subscription ISPs no longer offer particular advantages over free ones
Co-hosting	Server can run any of your scripts, but has access to an ISP's bandwidth	Expensive; in some circumstances server administration could be difficult
In house	Complete control over server, scripts and information	Can chew up bandwidth; responsibility for the server is the owner's

Making the connection

Once an ISP is chosen, the next step is how to link to the Net, which can be as simple as a modem hooked up to a single PC or as comprehensive as a leased line connected to a Local Area Network (**LAN**), as in Table 2.2.

Table 2.2   Options for connecting to the web

Connection type	Pros	Cons
Analog modem	Low cost; supported by every ISP	Slow; less reliable connection rates
ISDN	Effectively a dial-up leased line; instant and more reliable connection	Adapters and lines more expensive than modems; once online, may not be fast enough to justify the expense
ADSL	Faster than ISDN	Availability extremely limited; expensive
Cable	High speed with faster connection	Availability limited; speeds may decrease as more users come online
Leased line	Permanent connection; best way to connect to an in-house server	Very expensive

Analog   The most common type of link to the Internet, at least in terms of numbers of individuals, remains dial-up. While a 56Kb (kilobytes) per second modem may be more than sufficient for a home user, speed and reliability can become a real issue for more demanding users.

ISDN   ISDN (Integrated Services Digital Network) is effectively a leased line on demand, offering a theoretical dial-up connection of 64Kb, or even 128Kb, per second. ISDN connects more quickly than analog modems, but other bottlenecks such as slow servers or busy lines may affect data transfer.

Cable/ADSL   Fast alternatives to ISDN, including ADSL (Asymmetric Digital Subscriber Line) and cable modems, offer connections theoretically measured in Mb not Kb. ADSL offers a potential 2Mb per second link across a standard copper wire, but trials are limited and it remains expensive. Cable has made greater inroads in the UK, with a theoretical data transfer rate of 20Mb per second. In practice, cable modems are much slower because users share bandwidth with other users on a line. It is, however, considerably cheaper, with prices comparable to those for ISDN.

Leased line   All the above services are dial-up in one form or other, the alternative being a permanent connection best suited for businesses or institutions. Although one of the most expensive options, a flat fee of approximately £500 per month provides multiple-user access to a 64K voice and data line; larger bandwidth lines cost more. Another advantage of being connected via a leased line is that a web server can be set up much more easily.

PLANNING

Managing the project

Probably one area that is neglected when creating web pages is how to manage it as a project, but if a web site is to be a success resources must be allocated, deadlines observed and tasks established.

Anyone involved in project management will be presented with a job for which they have limited workers, time and resources. The first step in managing more effectively is to divide a complex project into essential tasks that can be assigned deadlines and set in order. More than this, however, successful project management requires allocating resources – whether money or workers – as well as providing warnings should these fall behind schedule.

In addition to ensuring that workers and time are allocated to meet a deadline, effective management should consider the consequences for deadlines and work if budgetary constraints are applied, for example how much work can be achieved if a certain amount of money is cut or moved elsewhere, or which tasks will have to be prioritised if deadlines are changed.

To make the process easier, a project can be divided into four distinct sections: defining the project, creating a project plan, tracking the project and then closing it. A project plan that maps out tasks and deadlines can be an indispensable tool for defining clearly the scope and resources available. The first step is to ensure that a realistic scope and deadlines for producing a web site are set, ensuring that assumptions can be met. To help with this, a project plan breaks the project down into tasks that can be assigned different resources and workers, having identified who or what will fulfil each task.

A project plan can proceed by one of two ways: a project start date is entered and the plan is scheduled forward to determine the best deadline, or the completion date is entered and tasks are scheduled backwards. Once people and resources are assigned to tasks, the essential building blocks, resources, need to be tracked, both to ensure that work is spread as evenly as possible and to plan for eventualities such as ill health or other work.

Closing a project is, typically, the successful delivery of a web site. However, one of the main mistakes made when creating an Internet or intranet site is failing to provide for its running costs, particularly in terms of time for maintenance. Consequently, closing a particular project may be establishing completion of the first stage, but will look forward to requirements and allocations for updates and managing the site.

Registering a domain name

While a web site may be hosted in a number of locations, determined principally by costs and technical support, one feature which is essential to make a mark on the web is a registered **domain name**, the web address that users type into their browser. Domain names are effectively the 'real estate' of the Internet, with easy-to-remember names being the virtual equivalent of prime-site addresses.

Domain names are registered with a non-profit body, the Internet Corporation for Assigned Names and Numbers (ICANN, www.icann.org), which holds a list of accredited registrars. Registration of domain names has become something of a business in its own right, with many entrepreneurial individuals and businesses engaging in a practice known as cybersquatting, buying up names that are likely to be requested and then charging a not-so-modest sum to transfer the name to a new owner. After several recent high-profile court cases, certain companies will no longer allow users to register commercial brand names or trademarks, although some Internet users and regulators are divided over this issue.

Many of the most obvious and best addresses (such as www.clickhere.com) have already been registered, as have phrases (www.coolsiteoftheday.com), but you can check whether a domain name is still available for registration at Nominet (www.nic.uk). You may even wish to reserve a domain name for which you do not yet have a web presence. By mid-1999, there were over 4.8 million domain names registered, a number that is growing at an estimated rate of 70,000 per week.

If the particular name you desire has already been snapped up, be inventive and consider possible variants of your name or the nature of your enterprise. When you find a combination that is still available, there are a few rules and tips that apply to registering a domain name:

TIPS FOR REGISTERING A DOMAIN NAME

- While certain key addresses (in particular bbc.co.uk) have made the .co.uk suffix popular in the UK, if your business is in any way international a .com address is advisable.

- If the domain name is part of a registered trademark or you want to prevent competitors using similar names to attract business, register as many variants (.com, .co.uk, .net) as possible.

- Domain names ending in the suffix .com are restricted to twenty-two or fewer characters. Those ending in .co.uk can have up to eighty characters.

- Letters, numbers, and hyphens can form part of a domain name, but not other characters or spaces.

- At the time of writing, the direct registration fee is approximately £40 per year for a .com address and £5 for a .co.uk address. These fees have to be renewed each year, and extra costs may be incurred for services such as redirecting email and hosting your web site (typically £100–£300 per year). Some sites, such as www.freenetname.co.uk, will register a .co.uk domain name free of charge.

The structure of a site

Part of the planning process requires the web producer to outline the site's structure, how information is to be distributed across pages. The structure of a site is important: like chapters in a book or an index, it serves a practical function both for the producer and for the visitor to the site. For the producer, having a clear idea of the site's structure can establish the parameters for the most important information, whether there should be a link to a particular area (information about a company or individual, for example) that is accessible from every part of the site. For the visitor, on the other hand, a clear site structure can be useful in navigating through pages.

The first page is typically referred to as the home page, the starting point for the visitor. Another key term is a portal: while, strictly speaking, a portal serves as a gateway to other areas and services on the Internet (the most famous portals being search engines such as Yahoo! and Excite), the entry point to a web site can itself be improved if it is conceived in terms of a gateway to that individual site. There are two choices here for the web designer: the first page may be a quick loading and relatively information-free starting point designed to load as soon as the visitor reaches the page, or it may offer as much information as possible about the site.

If the first page is a 'flag' page, for quick access, any links to the home page in the rest of the site should actually refer to another page that contains more useful and relevant information. One way around this is to include important links in a frame that is never updated, allowing visitors to navigate more quickly to other parts of the site. A common mistake is to provide a series of pages with minimal information (and probably loaded with advertisements) before reaching the important components of the site; while the temptation may be to keep visitors on a site for as long as possible, they are more likely to hit the back button on their browser.

After the portal or home page, a site is usually organised into 'top level' pages, which should represent the most logical organisation of a site. For example, a commercial web site may divide products into categories for sales, as well as provide support services and contacts. Top level pages should be available throughout the site, and do not represent the number of pages associated with a particular category: for example, individual products may constitute the main part of a site, but contacts, search engines and support links will also need to be clear.

As visitors navigate throughout the site, however, certain links to sections will become more relevant, others less so: if a visitor indicates a wish to read a sports section, for example, selecting between football, cricket and rugby suddenly becomes much more important than when reading the international affairs section.

A quick and easy way to indicate the structure of a site is to create a tree diagram that constellates pages around their logical order. While this can be done with flowchart software such as Visio, at the very least anyone responsible for web production should sketch out the main areas on paper before beginning work on building the site. Figure 2.2 is a diagram for the sample web site we will create in chapters four and five.

The web and commerce

While e-commerce did not arrive as quickly as some commentators predicted in the mid-1990s, since the end of that decade it has contributed

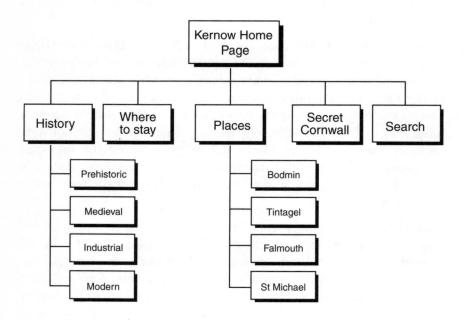

Figure 2.2   **A sample web site structure**

BUYING ONLINE

Certain companies have made considerable progress over the past couple of years in e-commerce. It is no surprise that computer hardware and software companies have taken to the Internet in droves, being the earliest adopters of e-commerce models. The computer manufacturer Dell (www.dell.com and www.dell.co.uk) claimed to be selling $1 million (£620,000) of equipment every day in 1997, rising to $18 million (£11 million) by 1999. Software sites such as Jungle.com (www.jungle.com) offer services to track sales once orders have been placed, and, to encourage purchases, many companies offer free delivery.

Another market growth area has been in books, CDs and films (including video and DVD). The trail blazed by Amazon (www.amazon.com and www.amazon.co.uk) has since been followed by a host of speculators, including BOL (www.bol.com) and CDNow (www.cdnow.com), but other services include supermarkets such as Tesco (www.tesco.co.uk) or Walmart (www.walmart.com) and ticket sales for events or holidays such as Microsoft's Expedia (www.expedia.com) and, as shown in Figure 2.3, lastminute.com (www.lastminute.com).

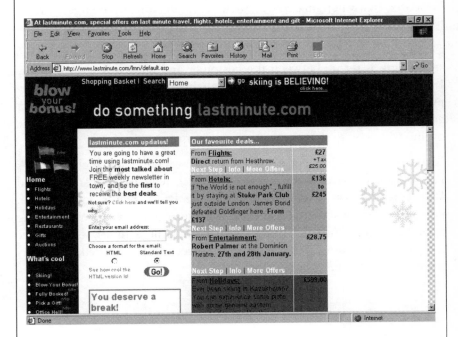

Figure 2.3 lastminute.com – one of many e-commerce sites launched in the UK

to renewed interest in the web. The Internet increasingly offers not only new levels of service and support for existing customers, but sales channels for new markets. It also serves as a platform for entirely new ventures, such as Amazon.com, an Internet sales outlet which shook major traditional booksellers such as Barnes and Noble and W. H. Smith, causing them to rethink their own online presence.

A key area, for example, where the Internet has been useful for businesses is as a supplement to mail-order services (where a database of products already exists in paper format). While creating an HTML catalogue with ordering support is increasingly simple, it may result in some operational difficulties which emphasise the importance of pre-production planning. Reaching a world-wide audience implies a 24-hour service, including customer support.

Those interested in setting up an e-commerce site that can process orders around the clock will require a payment processor and merchant agreement in order to accept credit card payments, such as those provided by Barclays Merchant Services (www.bms.barclays.co.uk) or NetBanx (www.netbanx.com). Such services typically charge start-up fees and a levy on each transaction that takes place.

Once a merchant agreement and payment processor are established, a secure link is set up between the customer and processor service: many ISPs offer support for this, but will probably charge extra. When information is sent to the processor, details are also passed to the customer and merchant that payment has been accepted, then transferred to the online company so that the order can be sent out.

Services with the aim of simplifying online commerce include IBM's Home Page Creator (www.ibm.com/hpc/uk), iCat (www.icat.com) and Web Street (www.webstreet.co.uk). Home Page creator, for example, provides a secure server and shopping basket with service costs ranging from £15 per month for Basic (twelve items at a time) to £120 per month for Premium (500 items); Web Street is more limited, but offers secure servers for £20 per month.

SETTING UP A TEST SITE

Locating the server

When producing a web site, you may wish to house your pages on an in-house or personal server or, more likely, an ISP site. Businesses or institutions with a leased line will have a fast and reliable connection to the Internet, with universities often having faster connections than many ISPs.

A leased line brings its own problems, however. Using such a system does not simply consist of buying a modem and hooking it into a network: to redirect traffic from a LAN across the Internet requires a **router** and, because such a system is connected to the Internet twenty-four hours a day, it is more vulnerable to hackers, making a **firewall** advisable. A firewall is a piece of hardware or a specially configured computer through which an Internet connection is filtered to prevent unwanted attempts to bring down or infiltrate the network.

The vast majority of web producers will not be responsible for actually setting up and maintaining the server, this being the responsibility of an IT department, but it is still advisable to learn as much as you can about the operating system that you are using, particularly if you are responsible for administering and maintaining a site. In particular, dynamic web services require scripts or programs to be hosted on the server, and for this reason it is advisable to set up a test server on which you can run scripts.

Such a server can be as complex as a separate box on a network or a personal server running on the same computer used to design web pages. UNIX forms the basis on which the Internet was built, with Windows NT gradually being offered by more and more ISPs because of the demand for FrontPage Extensions support. Another system that is gaining a lot of attention recently is **Linux**, not simply because it is free (as in 'free speech', not 'free beer') but also because it has a reputation for being robust and was designed from the ground up as a UNIX clone and networking solution.

Setting up a server

While it is possible to develop a web site without using a server to test your design, some features of web production cannot be tested without a server. In addition, if you are to be responsible for managing an Internet or intranet web site, using a test web server can prevent problems later on.

Setting up a server can be a complicated task, and we will look briefly at setting up a network box using the Microsoft Internet Information Server (IIS) and a UNIX-based server such as Apache. More common is the requirement to test certain features such as server-generated responses or FrontPage extensions, for which you can use a stand-alone server such as the Microsoft Personal Web Server (**PWS**). For many requirements this will be sufficient, as some advanced features offered by IIS, such as support for **ASP** (Active Server Pages) and FrontPage extensions are also supported by PWS.

Setting up a network is rather beyond the scope of this book. There are some factors, however, that you should consider before setting up a small test network. In contrast to a large company or institutional network that has a dedicated IP address and permanent connection to the Internet, it is possible to set up a network that uses different TCP/IP settings for the local area network as opposed to the dial-up settings that operate via a modem.

Certain addresses are 'reserved' for private use rather than connecting to the Internet, including 10.0.0.0 to 10.255.255.255, 172.16.0.0 to 172.31.255.255 and 192.168.0.0. If you set IP addresses on computers on a LAN to one of these ranges, even if one of these 'escapes' to the Internet it will not affect any servers. Another address, particularly useful for testing sites being hosted and developed on a stand-alone machine is the 'loopback' address, 127.0.0.1, which addresses its requests to the current machine and does not require the computer's actual IP address.

Microsoft IIS on NT

Microsoft Internet Information Server is a very powerful server which is free with Windows NT Server and provides services for web, FTP and database access. If you are using NT that is set up as a file server across a network, but is not running IIS, this can be set up by going to Start, Programs, Microsoft Internet Server, Internet Information Server Setup.

IIS installs several components: the Internet Service Manager, world wide web services and samples, gopher and FTP services. It also sets up the directories for these services to be published to, usually C:\InetPub\wwwroot and so on. The server uses the TCP/IP settings provided for the network adapter, so the final step of installation is to test the server using another machine on the network. In the browser, type in the IP address or the server name: if the server is running correctly, the browser will display the Internet Information Server home page.

If IIS is not running, this is probably because several of the services have not been automatically started. To engage these services, you must go to Start, Programs, Administrative Tools, Server Manager and, from the window that appears, select Computer, Services. A list appears which includes FTP, web and gopher services if these have been installed correctly: clicking Start will begin these services, but they can also be set up to run automatically by selecting Startup and ensuring that Automatic is the chosen option.

Apache on Linux

Even if you are using a small network or an individual machine, you can still employ Linux (www.linux.org) to run one of the most popular web servers around, Apache (www.apache.org), to host a test site. Apache was derived from the NCSA server, the primary server developed to host web sites which forms the basis for most server specifications on the Internet. Because of Linux's excellent support of technologies that were developed for UNIX, such as scripting, and the fact that the majority of ISPs use Apache, Linux can provide an inexpensive test environment.

Because of its open source nature, Linux comes in different flavours provided by companies such as Calder, Red Hat, SuSE and Slackware. As with NT, it is possible to set up a 'safe' IP address, or to use the loopback address 127.0.0.1 if Linux is not on a network. When Apache is installed, the server root is set by default in a directory such as /usr/local/httpd or usr/local/etc/httpd; navigating to this directory will reveal directories for documents and scripts.

Once Apache is up and running, connecting to the server from a remote computer on the network should display the Apache home page. The server can be accessed via the same software used to publish pages to the web (see 'Managing UNIX sites' in chapter six).

Microsoft Personal Web Server

While Apache and IIS require considerable technical skill to set up a network and administer the web server, a more common requirement is to run a server on the computer where the web site is being produced in order to test certain features which cannot be run from the browser alone. There are several personal web servers which are fairly simple to set up, such as WebQuest Web Server, but probably the most commonly used is the Microsoft Personal Web Server, particularly as it is bundled with applications such as FrontPage and Windows 98.

If you are using Windows 98, this web server can be installed from the CD; if you do not have the Windows 98 CD, PWS can be downloaded from www.microsoft.com/windows/ie/pws. During installation, PWS sets up a default root directory for world wide web services and this is where the home page is found. To work with web pages, the Personal Web Server should load when Windows starts, and place an icon in the system tray in the bottom right corner of the taskbar. If it does not load, it needs to be started from Start, Programs, Internet Explorer, Personal Web Server, and Start clicked to make items available on a web site.

From the Personal Web Server, directories can be added to a web site for different users, and this is where properties such as access and the ability to browse directories are set. Once PWS is up and running, web pages that are copied into the root web directory can be viewed via a web browser. If the part of the file address up to wwwroot, such as file:///C|/Internet/wwwroot, or C:\Internet\wwwroot, is replaced with http://127.0.0.1, then the page will reload with active, server-side information being pushed from PWS rather than called by the browser, with the result that certain features such as scripts and databases will be displayed, rather than saved elsewhere on the hard drive.

3
Online media toolkit

One of the virtues of producing for the web is that, in comparison with other media such as print and broadcasting, it can be very inexpensive once you have the basic equipment in the form of a personal computer and a modem. With the price of computers falling all the time and 'free' ISPs becoming more prevalent, it is possible to create sophisticated pages with little more than the text editor bundled with the operating system.

While it is possible to build a web site with nothing more than the tools included with an operating system, in practice producers will employ other programs, many of which are aimed to simplify the task of hand-coding a web site, others providing support for tasks such as video or image editing. There is a thriving market in tools to help web producers, many of them available as freeware or shareware on the web (shareware programs are distributed freely but require users to register if the application is used after the evaluation period).

This chapter will outline the essential 'toolkit' for online production: not every application listed here is required – video on the web, for example, still tends to be a specialised requirement – but the aim of this chapter is to be as comprehensive as possible. In addition to listing shareware and professional applications, this chapter will introduce some of the terminology and techniques that every web producer should know about.

WEB PLATFORMS AND HTML

Browsers

After hardware, the first requirement for using the web involves the browser which, as such software becomes more complex, raises the system requirements for computers. There are two main web platforms, Netscape Communicator (incorporating Navigator) and Microsoft Internet Explorer. Since late 1995, these two competitors have been slugging it out to achieve market dominance. At the time of writing, Netscape remains the most popular browser, owing particularly to its excellent cross-platform support, but Microsoft has used its position as the largest software manufacturer to bring Internet Explorer into close second.

These so-called 'browser wars' have considerable consequences for web production and usage. While some commentators have welcomed such competition as stimulating development, the fact that browsers can interpret HTML in slightly different ways – even introducing proprietary tags – means that pages may display differently depending on whether the viewer uses Explorer or Communicator.

It is easy to assume that everyone uses either Communicator or Internet Explorer, and the web statistics service, The Counter (www.the-counter.com) claims that of some 270 million impressions recorded, over 85 per cent were via Internet Explorer and Communicator 4 or above. Nonetheless, there are alternatives, either in the form of new browsers such as Opera (www.operasoftware.com) or people with low-powered machines surfing the web with older versions of IE, Navigator or even Mosaic.

The important point for producers is that content on the web cannot be controlled in its final format in the same way that print or broadcast programs can be specified: the web browser used by the end viewer will affect the final product, and a considerable amount of time can be spent by developers testing their pages across a wide range of browsers. It may even be the case that two versions of a site are produced, one incorporating the latest effects, the other being a text-only site.

Testing a site, therefore, can be extremely important, and probably the first part of a toolkit the web producer should invest in is as many different browsers as possible. While this book will cover issues of cross-browser compatibility, however, there will always be times, when using particular plug-ins or effects, when a choice will have to be made between compatibility for as wide an audience as possible and demonstrating a particular technology or using it for a specific effect. For example, the accompanying web site for this book, www.producing.routledge.com, is designed to work with all browsers capable of displaying images and basic tables (such as Navigator 2); it does not look as aesthetically pleasing in such browsers, but text and links are displayed. The sample site that you will create in chapters four and five, however, will only work properly in version 3.0 browsers, and some features will not work in anything less than a version 4.0 browser.

HTML

HTML (hypertext markup language) is the coding language used to create documents on the web, the core component of any web page. Rather than being a full (and therefore complex) programming language, HTML employs tags indicated by angular brackets, for example <TITLE>, to surround text codes: these tags are interpreted by a browser such as Mosaic, Navigator or Internet Explorer, which control how the page appears. Usually there is an opening and a closing tag, the latter including a forward slash, such as </TITLE>, to indicate when a particular tag ends. More importantly, HTML allows you to create documents that link to other documents on the web – hence hypertext.

HTML tags may also include attributes that change the properties of a component on a web page; our title, for example, may include the attribute ALIGN="center" to align it with the middle of a page.

HTML is defined by the World Wide Web Consortium (www.w3c.org) that sets certain standards governing how code can be viewed by any browser on any computer in the world. HTML 2.0 is an older standard: consequently, it is less sophisticated than versions 3.2 and 4.0 but is capable of being interpreted by older browsers. HTML 4.0 implements support for advanced scripting and better navigation and search capabilities, but pages designed for HTML 4.0 compatible browsers may not display as intended on earlier browsers.

One of the biggest choices facing web designers is how far to move away from raw HTML when designing web pages. Most new users have no interest at all in hand-coding – after all, print designers do not need to understand PostScript to lay out pages for high-end printing processes. Nonetheless, although visual editors have increased in sophistication over recent years, a working knowledge of HTML is still recommended as even the best editors occasionally make mistakes with code that are easier to rectify if you have some knowledge of HTML.

Code: first encounters

If you use the View Source menu option in a browser, you can see the HTML code that formats a page. Throughout the rest of the book, when describing various design effects that you can achieve with different editors and applications, there will also be descriptions of how to accomplish the same task by using a text editor and raw HTML. For further information, consult the HTML reference at the back of this book; and there is a fuller introductory course to programming in HTML on the web site at www.producing.routledge.com/techniques.htm.

In the meantime, you may wish to get started with HTML coding with the following, simple page. To create web pages this way, all you need is a simple text editor, such as Notepad on the PC or SimpleText on the Mac. While you can use other word processors, you need to save the final file as text-only format to prevent any formatting used by the word processor, and incomprehensible to a web browser, being included in your web page.

When you have opened your text editor, enter the following code:

```
<HTML>
<HEAD>
   <TITLE>Hello World </TITLE>
</HEAD>
<BODY>
   <HR>
   <CENTER>
   <H1>Hello World! Simple HTML</H1>
   </CENTER>
   <HR><P>
   <H2>Your first web page</H2><P>
   As with a word processor, there are times when
you want to <I>emphasise</I> certain words or
<U>underline</U> a specific point. These are some
of the simplest elements to make your page look
<B>bolder</B> in all the right places.<P>
</BODY>
</HTML>
```

Save the above file as hello.htm (rather than with another extension, such as .doc or .txt) and then open it in your browser. You should see a page with simple text formatting including bold, italic and underline and two different types of heading <H1> and <H2>. If elements are missing from your page, check that you have included both sets of tags.

Browsers actually work very well even if some of these tags are in the wrong place, so that an <IMG> tag in the <HEAD> ... </HEAD> section will still be displayed on the page. Likewise, if you create a meaningless tag such as <RUBBISH JOEBLOGGS="Hello world"> the browser will simply ignore it. This is one of the reasons why the web has developed so rapidly, as older browsers ignore new tags (with some exceptions). In addition, HTML is not case sensitive, so while all examples in this book are written in capitals to distinguish them, you do not need to do this when modifying your own code – though it can make it easier to find tags at a later date.

Code editors such as HomeSite offer tools to help producers work with HTML, for example colour to indicate different elements of the language and indents to make them easier to read. If you are hand-coding a page with a simple text editor, some of these may be impossible to implement, but it is still useful to indent different levels of code to make items easier to find. You can also include comments to identify sections of a page using two forward slashes, as in <//Copy this section>, so that the comment will not be displayed by the browser.

EDITING PACKAGES

Web editors

While we have discussed HTML, unless you wish to work very slowly (and very carefully) when creating a web site, you are unlikely to produce web pages using a text editor alone. First of all, page design often involves the use of such things as **JavaScript**, Dynamic HTML (**DHTML**), **ActiveX** and Cascading Style Sheets (**CSS**) that can be very complex when typing in a text editor. While inserting images and hyperlinks is, in most cases, straightforward, hand-coding something like a table is more likely to create a headache than anything usable.

Unlike DTP or image editing, dominated by Quark XPress and Adobe PhotoShop respectively, because of the open nature of HTML there is no clear market leader: at the time of writing, Dreamweaver is probably the single most important package that employers look for, but everything it does can be achieved in other packages.

In addition, unlike print, where the producer distributes a version over which they have had more or less complete control, a web producer cannot guarantee the system on which their pages are to be displayed. This means that if a visitor does not have the font on your page installed on their computer, text will return to the visitor's default (such as Times New Roman), which will cause text to reflow in boxes on a page. One way to escape this difficulty in transferring documents electronically is by using a format such as Adobe's Portable Document Format (**PDF**), which embeds fonts and images within a page; doing this, however, can mean that visitors without Adobe Acrobat installed may not view your site.

A more common way of controlling some of the vagaries of design is to employ tables to lay out components of a page, and all current editors support this feature while most can also use frames and some style sheets which can simplify the web designer's task. Another element of web production that is not always addressed adequately is site management, but whereas only a few years ago this was something of a rarity, more and more applications now have in-built management features.

Below are some of the most common web editors: this list is by no means exhaustive, but covers virtually all the major commercial applications and some of the most successful shareware applications (see Table 3.1). Each one is accompanied by a description outlining its strengths and weaknesses, as well as its intended level of use. For a more comprehensive list, consult the *Producing for the Web* site.

Adobe GoLive   Originally GoLive's CyberStudio, this application gained a great deal of support in the Mac and is now available for the PC as well as the Mac. GoLive 5 includes an enhanced link manager for site control and pixel level page layout control. There is good support for more advanced features of web design, such as scripting, DHTML and cascading style sheets (CSS). GoLive's approach is slightly different from that of other editors: in addition to a visual editor it also offers a 'tabbed' view of HTML code similar to that in HoTMetaL Pro for designers wishing to edit tags quickly. Its main competitor is probably

Dreamweaver, demonstrating some strengths (such as animation support) and some failings (site structure control) compared to that program.

Adobe PageMill   PageMill 3, is a web page and site designer available for the PC and Mac and aimed at users with little or no experience of web production. Site management and page creation have been simplified greatly, imitating as much as possible a DTP application. Rather than having to specify tables and positions, the designer can insert images and type anywhere on the page. For more advanced features, components such as ActiveX elements and Java can be added to a page, but users wishing to create something more complex must be prepared to write the code. An easy way of creating individual pages and handling uncomplicated sites, PageMill is really only recommended for beginners rather than advanced users.

Allaire HomeSite   HomeSite 4 is really an HTML text editor with some added visual features for page design and site management. The default view is of colour-coded HTML, but it is also possible to transfer to a visual design view of pages. This particular application is aimed more at technical users, particularly those who wish to achieve more complex things in HTML. HomeSite's apparent strength lies in its support for the advanced aspects of HTML, such as scripting, ASP and DHTML, but these largely consist of useful tags for entering your own scripts, which is little more than what other programs offer. It remains, however, a first-class text editor.

Arachnophilia   Arachnophilia is a free web editor and one of the longest survivors, currently being up to version 3.9. Unlike many editors it is very compact, the download file being 1.5Mb, and it works as a text rather than a visual editor, highlighting tags in different colours to enable producers to edit them quickly. It can also be used to edit **Perl, CGI** (common gateway interface) scripts and even high-level programming languages such as C++ and Java text very easily, with buttons and menus to add components to a page. There are also wizards for creating such things as tables, which can be very confusing to code by hand.

Filemaker Home Page Another web editor for beginners on the Mac or PC, Home Page 3 makes creating a site very easy but is also very limited. Users can produce a web site using a wizard or a template, but the options available are rather restricted. One good feature, which can speed up production considerably, is that by building a library elements such as graphics and text can be added to pages simply by dragging and dropping them from a library window. Basic site management is provided, essentially a list view of your files from where you can check for broken links.

Macromedia Dreamweaver An extremely sophisticated editor, Dreamweaver 3 is probably the closest thing there is to a standard in terms of web design. Pages can be edited entirely in visual mode, and Dreamweaver makes a very good job of making page design as close to DTP as possible. The program uses a series of floating palettes and windows, which can be fairly confusing for a novice although it can incorporate everything from JavaScript buttons to Flash and Java **applets**. As well as first-class management and automation tools, where Dreamweaver excels is in its support for scripting. While requiring some experience to use effectively, it is possible to add JavaScript rollovers, pop-up windows and DHTML animations with no hand-coding at all. The power of Dreamweaver lies in the fact that it supports advanced features as if they were basic: its interface is not the simplest to use, but it is currently the best editor around.

McWeb Software Web Weaver Web Weaver 98 is a shareware text editor that, like HotDog and Arachnophilia, has been around for some time and built up a considerable following, employing toolbars to add common components to pages. It also supports HTML 4.0, although not dynamic HTML elements, with wizards for such things as adding frames. The slightly more expensive 'gold' version includes a site-management tool, 'Site Mongrel', and a CGI script to analyse web-site usage.

Microsoft FrontPage FrontPage 2000 is a powerful web editor that, aside from a couple of points, is also easy to use. It includes many features specific to the Microsoft Internet Information Server (IIS) bundled with Windows NT, which is beginning to be supported by more and more ISPs. In addition, a cut-down and easier-

to-use version is included with Internet Explorer 4 and above, so
many web producers experiment with FrontPage before migrating
to another editor. To make full use of FrontPage extensions, you
will need a server installed to view them. Site-management features are fairly extensive, and you can view your site as a map or a
visual display of links. There is also support for advanced features
such as scripting and DHTML.

Microsoft FrontPage Express   Included as part of Internet Explorer,
FrontPage Express is now up to version 2. While it includes some
of the features of FrontPage, it is in fact a completely separate
editor. Users of Microsoft Word will find FrontPage Express
extremely easy to use, sharing many of the same toolbars and buttons, and for stand-alone pages it offers most elements that a producer will require, including form components but no frames. It
also does not provide the dynamic HTML features of FrontPage
2000, essentially being an HTML 3.2 editor, nor are there management features. As a free editor, it's good for beginners.

NetObjects Fusion   Rather than present the user with a prolifera-
tion of toolbars, Fusion 5 offers a Control Bar and Standard Tools
Bar as well as a context-sensitive properties palette. The aim of
Fusion is to simplify web design by standardising layout techniques, as well as to offer decent web-management tools. The
Page view is where you lay out your designs and Site view the
spot from where you create links and add new pages, with a Style
section to speed up development. A problem with the application
is that it is extremely difficult to edit your files in raw HTML if
you need to (they are not saved in HTML format until published), but, as with Dreamweaver, it is possible to create
JavaScript buttons and effects without any programming knowledge.

Netscape Composer   Composer was first added to version 3 of
Netscape Navigator Gold, but is now available as part of
Netscape Communicator. Like FrontPage Express, it is a basic
visual web editor supporting HTML 3.2 and works in a manner
very similar to a word processor. Again, as with its competitor
from Microsoft, it is a stand-alone page editor and omits certain
features, such as frame support; another difficulty is that there are

no form tools. What upgrades there have been over the past few years have been gimmicks rather than truly useful additions, such as the ability to create 'rainbow text', but the widespread use of Navigator means that it is more likely to produce pages that can be read across a number of computer platforms.

Sausage Software HotDog   The unlikely-titled HotDog has been around for a long time, and although it is offered as shareware Hot-Dog 5.5 is one of the most feature-rich text editors around. HotDog Express is a freely available beginner's package, but Hot-Dog Professional includes toolbars and SuperToolz to add such things as DHTML and HTML 4.0 components to a page. There is also a HotDog Webmaster suite available. The program includes a preview window (Rover) which displays the page as you add HTML components. While it is possible to do every-thing that HotDog offers in a simple text editor such as Notepad, like the best text web editors it simplifies many complex and powerful features.

SoftQuad HoTMetaL Pro   HoTMetaL Pro 6 provides a graphical editor and, like GoLive, can also display the HTML tags, indicat-ing where the editor inserts code in response to the user's actions. Site-management features are excellent, providing a diagram-matic view of links and pages that can be scrolled through, indi-cating immediately clusters of links. HoTMetaL also includes a very useful validation tool: if this is left on, code is flagged as soon as you enter an element that may not be cross-browser com-patible, and it makes HoTMetaL a useful tool for checking pages designed in other editors. On the whole, however, this demands more technical expertise than the other visual designers.

CREATING GRAPHICS

An essential tool for any web designer is an application to handle images: with some exceptions, probably most time spent on site devel-opment after producing copy is in creating graphics. Until very recently, PCs were from Mars and Macs were from Venus – and any poor earth-bound computer user had to travel out in entirely different directions depending on which package they wished to use. For graphics artists, there was only one choice: the Mac, every time.

Table 3.1   Web editors

Program	Platform	Editor type	Site manager	Contact	Typical price
Adobe GoLive 5	PC/Mac	Visual/text	Yes	www.adobe.com	£200
Adobe PageMill 3	PC/Mac	Visual	Yes	www.adobe.com	£75
Allaire HomeSite 4	PC/Mac	Text	Yes	www.unipalm.com	£95
Arachnophilia 3.9	PC	Text	No	www.arachnoid.com	Free
Filemaker Home Page 3	PC/Mac	Visual	Yes	www.filemaker.com	£75
McWeb Web Weaver 98	PC	Text	Yes (gold only)	www.mcwebsoft-ware.com	$29.95/ $34.95 gold
Macromedia Dreamweaver 3	PC/Mac	Visual/text	Yes	www.macromedia.com	£265
Microsoft FrontPage 2000	PC	Visual/text	Yes	www.microsoft.com	£110
Microsoft FrontPage Express 2	PC/Mac	Visual	No	www.microsoft.com	Free
NetObjects Fusion 5	PC	Visual	Yes	www.netobjects.com	£335
Netscape Composer	PC/Mac	Visual	No	www.netscape.com	Free
Sausage Software HotDog 5.5	PC	Text	Yes (Professional)	www.sausage.com	$130
SoftQuad HoTMetaL Pro 6	PC	Visual/text	Yes	www.softquad.com	£110

With the introduction of Windows 95, however, competition has increased: many of the best applications are designed first for the Mac, but the ports quickly appear for Windows. The Mac is still the chosen platform, but this is as much to do with the cumulative skills base of graphics designers working on Apple computers as any question of quality with regard to the PC. The image editors outlined below and in Table 3.2 concentrate mainly on cross-platform applications, as well as some shareware packages principally for Windows, but there are freeware editors, such as GIMP for Linux, which are also very powerful.

Image basics

There are two basic steps involved in capturing a digital image: sampling and quantisation. Differing intensities are sampled at a grid location and then quantised to pixel values on the screen, that is the intensity is calculated in terms of brightness of red, green and blue, and the result approximated to a number, or digital value.

This two-stage process is known as filtering. Another way to think of filtering, especially when used in scanning techniques, is of a finger sensing Braille dots at regular points on the surface before translating these dots into a coherent image. These digital values produced by filtering are then displayed as pixels. Each pixel is a discrete element of a picture, similar to the dots that you see in a newspaper photo if you look at it through a strong magnifying glass. The quality of the image depends largely on the sampling grid so that if it is too coarse valuable detail will be irretrievably lost.

Yet infinitely fine detail is unworkable across the web. An 8" × 10" monochrome print at 600 dots per inch (dpi) requires 4,800 × 6,000, or 28,800,800, pixels to appear completely smooth – approximately 3.6Mb; to record the same image in 256-shade greyscale requires 28.8Mb uncompressed storage space, and 24-bit colour (with eight bits per pixel for red, green and blue, offering a potential 16.7 million colours) would require 86.4Mb, or the equivalent of 500 copies of this book's text.

For images displayed on screen, resolutions are much lower, between 75 and 92 dpi. Similarly, compression of up to a half can be achieved with no loss of image quality, and compression between 1/10 and 1/50 can be achieved with no perceptible loss of quality. The reason for this is that an image will contain many of the same colours that can be described by a more compact algorithm; because no image can have more shades of colour than number of pixels (and very few images have as many as 16.7 million pixels), colours can be mapped onto palettes to save space.

Another distinction when dealing with graphics is between **bitmap**, or photographic images, and **vector** illustrations, or drawings. While bitmap, or raster, images work by recording information about each pixel in an illustration, vector images use equations to describe the position and direction of lines on a screen. Thus, whereas a bitmap may have to describe each pixel that constitutes a line, a vector is defined in terms of two points and the distance between them.

The two main image types used on the web are **JPEG** (Joint Photographic Experts Group) and **GIF** (Graphic Interchange Format) images, although there are other formats: some, such as the Flash vector format, proprietary, others such as **PNG** (Portable Network Graphics), open standards that can be displayed by the latest browsers without plug-ins. GIF images are restricted to 256 colours but are better at displaying large areas of a single colour, whereas JPEG files employ higher compression rates and display more colours, making them more suitable for photographic images.

Applications

Adobe Illustrator One of the great-grandparents of the design world, Illustrator 9 from Adobe has long been the vector drawing package of choice for many graphic designers. Illustrator is really intended as the drawing companion to PhotoShop, with this program providing the tools to produce very complex objects, from basic shapes such as polygons and curls to controlling gradient colour fills.

Adobe ImageReady Designed to be used with PhotoShop, and sporting the same interface, ImageReady 2 is Adobe's image editor aimed at the web. With ImageReady you can slice images to optimise file sizes, and it supports GIF, JPEG and PNG-8/PNG-24 file formats for the web. The program also uses layers to create frames for animation, with the final result being saved as an animated GIF.

Adobe PhotoShop PhotoShop remains the de facto standard for image professionals, and with version 5.5 Adobe has introduced extra support for optimising file formats for the web. A new feature is the Save For Web window, which displays up to four previews of a graphic at different compression rates, so that it is easier to judge the trade-off between size and quality.

CorelDRAW! The essentials of CorelDRAW! 9 are the eponymous vector illustration package and its bitmap editor, PhotoPAINT, in addition to some other utilities such as CorelTRACE for converting bitmaps to vector images. Creating graphics has been made progressively easier with each release of DRAW, via such things as the Template Wizard, and it has a fairly intelligent (if overwhelming) interface. PhotoPAINT converts layers and images into masks that are easier to work with than similar layers in PhotoShop.

Jasc Paint Shop Pro Paint Shop Pro was originally a great success on the PC as shareware, and version 6 offers vector image editing in conjunction with bitmap editing, presenting an application that is, for the vast majority of people, nearly as comprehensive as PhotoShop for a fraction of the price. The main virtue of Paint Shop Pro is that it flips easily between vector and bitmap drawing styles and supports a wide range of image formats, making it a good general image editor for the web.

Macromedia Fireworks   Fireworks 3 is an image editing package that concentrates on optimising graphics for the web, using some clever tricks to slice images to compress them as much as possible, and offering a host of special effects, including animations, as well as rollover buttons and the ability to create image maps. Fireworks has been designed principally for screen- rather than print-based graphics, and its interface is similar to that of Dreamweaver, which it is intended to complement.

Macromedia Freehand   If you are looking for a dedicated vector-based drawing package the choice probably still remains between Freehand and Illustrator. Freehand 9 integrates with Macromedia's other Internet tools such as Fireworks, Director and Flash.

Metacreations Painter   Painter 6 uses 'natural media' tools for re-creating watercolour, oils, pencil, pen, and brush effects, as well as 'canvases', paper and cloth grains that react and blend to produce more subtle changes when used with different brushes such as chalk, paint and charcoal. Though these have been imitated by other image editors, along with its cloning tools, Painter remains one of the most sophisticated packages around.

NetGraphics Studio   A wizard-driven optimiser to get the most from your graphics, this is a cheap tool for use with other bitmap editors. NetGraphics Studio 2 takes users step by step through the process to optimise images, such as cropping, dithering and saving in web-safe colours, and there is also a useful batch export tool.

WebPainter   Much cheaper than many other bitmap editors, WebPainter 3.0 can be purchased online from Totally Hip Software and includes a wide range of image creation and animation tools.

Table 3.2 Image editors

Program	Platform	Type	Animation	Contact	Typical price
Adobe Illustrator 9	PC/Mac	Vector	Yes (Flash)	www.adobe.com	£295
Adobe ImageReady 2	PC/Mac	Bitmap	Yes[1]	www.adobe.com	£110
Adobe PhotoShop 5.5	PC/Mac	Bitmap	Yes	www.adobe.com	£500
CorelDRAW! 9	PC/Mac	Vector/bitmap	No	www.corel.com	£310
Jasc PaintShop Pro 6	PC	Vector/bitmap	No	www.jasc.com	£95
Macromedia Fireworks 3	PC/Mac	Bitmap	Yes	www.macromedia.com	£160
Macromedia Freehand 9	PC/Mac	Vector	Yes (Flash)	www.macromedia.com	£350
MetaCreations Painter 6	PC/Mac	Bitmap	Yes	www.metacreations.com	£320
NetGraphics Studio 2	PC	Bitmap	No	www.hemera.com	£60
WebPainter 3.0	PC	Bitmap	Yes	www.totallyhip.com	$89.95

Note
1 via ImageReady 2, bundled with version 5.5

INTERACTIVITY AND CGI

Most of the pages encountered on the web are static, effectively consisting of pages that could be used in print medium with the exception of the occasional animated GIF and hyperlinks. Interactivity on such sites comes from navigation controls and links, but more extensive interactivity can be provided in the form of changing elements in response to user input, such as search results from a database, modified displays when the mouse moves over parts of the page such as rollovers or drop-down menus, or sections of a page that can be moved around by the user.

Links aside, interactivity on the web generally doesn't come from HTML but rather from a number of languages and external objects that are embedded into pages, including JavaScript, CGI, Java applets, cascading style sheets, **Shockwave/Flash** components and dynamic HTML.

While static pages do not take full advantage of the web, it is worth hesitating a moment before rushing to the other extreme and adding alert boxes or Java image applets simply because you can. For a start, such elements, especially if poorly designed, can slow down loading times; more than this, however, if they are overused and pointless, they may interfere with a site's overall design.

Dynamic HTML

Dynamic HTML is an important step for the next generation of HTML, but also an indication of the potential pitfalls that occur when competitors struggle to establish a proprietary rather than open standard. Both Netscape and Microsoft browsers support DHTML in their latest versions, but each uses a slightly different version, meaning that DHTML produced for Internet Explorer is not necessarily compatible with Navigator's.

In its broadest sense, dynamic HTML brings together cascading style sheets and scripting tools, promising a finer degree of control over screen layout, more impressive interactivity and advanced multimedia features, and layered documents.

What DHTML does is introduce a series of tags that enable designers to control JavaScript and CSS elements on the fly, for example drop-down menus or hidden sections of a page. Dynamic HTML has the potential to be an extremely effective interactive multimedia language – it is, for example, much quicker than Java – but its adoption has been hindered by cross-browser compatibility. What this means for current designers is that they must often limit access to a site to one browser, produce two versions of the same site, whether for different versions of DHTML or one version with and one without DHTML, or, more commonly, ignore it until compatibility issues are resolved.

Cascading style sheets

Cascading style sheets (CSS) enable designers to specify the appearance of pages through control of the elements contained within them, for example to display all level-two headings a particular colour. There are two specifications for cascading style sheets, CSS1 and CSS2, which control text formatting and positioning respectively. To incorporate a style into a page requires the <STYLE> ... </STYLE> tag with declarations and properties separated by a colon within curly braces, for example:

```
<STYLE TYPE="text/css">
H2 {color:blue}
</STYLE>
```

The reason these are called 'cascading' style sheets is that they can be nested one inside another, with the one closest to the destination having most control. If a page was to have one paragraph in the Arial font, for example, it would look something as follows:

```
<P STYLE="font-family:Arial">This paragraph in
Arial font.</P>
```

As the main use of CSS is to define overall styles for a site, the easiest way to use it is not to cut and paste into every page, but use the <LINK> tag in the header of a page to connect to an externally referenced style sheet, such as <LINK REL=STYLESHEET TYPE="text/css" HREF="pages/style1">.

Layers

Style sheets can provide an overall definition of a site's appearance, but the most exciting potential development of dynamic HTML is layering – and the most disappointing because IE and Communicator implement different types of layering. Layers using the Communicator <LAYER> tag indicate the absolute position of a component using x and y co-ordinates relative to the left and top of the browser window.

Layering not only allows a component to be positioned anywhere on screen without using tabs and carriage returns, thus improving the appearance of a page, but also places layers one above the other. Not only can elements be positioned over others, they can be made visible or invisible, creating tabbed pages, for example, that display different contents as visitors click on each tab.

JavaScript

Scripting is a way to extend the capabilities of HTML, particularly for dynamic feedback, the most popular version being JavaScript. This was originally developed by Netscape (under the name of LiveScript) but didn't really take off until Sun Microsystems took part in development and it was renamed JavaScript. JavaScript is recognised by most browsers currently in use, although versions of Internet Explorer prior to version 4 used Microsoft's VBScript and a variant of JavaScript called Jscript. Indeed, there remain some incompatibilities between Microsoft and Netscape implementations of JavaScript, but these are less serious than differences in DHTML, and JavaScript is the most widely supported scripting language in use today.

HTML uses the tag <SCRIPT> ... </SCRIPT> to include scripts in a page, which allows compatibility with both today's languages and any future ones, as indicated by the attribute LANGUAGE. Such scripts are interpreted by the browser and are part of a client-side process, rather than server-side CGI. Including JavaScript in a browser is very easy, although creating the script itself may be more difficult.

```
<HEAD>
<SCRIPT LANGUAGE="JavaScript">
<!-- hide script
"Insert your script here"
// stop hiding script -->
</SCRIPT>
</HEAD>
```

If you were using another scripting language such as VBScript (only supported by IE), the LANGUAGE attribute would need to be changed in the above example. Everything between <!-- and --> is ignored by browsers that are not JavaScript compliant.

JavaScript is an object-oriented program, which means that every element on a page, such as images, forms and headings, can be defined as an object and named; once such objects are indicated, their properties can be changed so that, for example, check-boxes can be 'checked' or image paths changed to substitute them for other graphics (the principle behind rollover buttons). JavaScript also employs 'methods', or commands, to cause certain actions to occur on a certain event, such as a mouse click. For more information, see the JavaScript examples in chapter four.

XML and XSL

HTML has developed greatly since it was introduced at the beginning of the 1990s, and is increasingly being used to achieve tasks for which it was not originally designed, ranging from creating help files to providing common file formats for such things as word-processed documents. Recognising the shortcomings of HTML compared to these new uses, the World Wide Web Consortium introduced eXtensible Markup Language (**XML**) as a replacement for the stop-gap Meta tags that had been used to extend HTML functionality.

XML is closely related to **SGML** (Standard Generalised Markup Language) and provides web documents with the ability to be self-describing, whereby new tags are created rather like fields in a database. Thus the line <H1>Frankfurt</H1> is recognised by HTML as a heading, but could be either the city or a sausage; using XML, the tag <Location> can be defined to indicate the type of information contained in this tag, and this information then used with an **XSL** style sheet to display different types of information, rather like cascading style sheets.

XML is actually a combination of three technologies: the eXtensible Markup Language itself, eXtensible Style Language (XSL) style sheet descriptions and Document Type Definitions (DTD) that enable XML documents to be passed between applications and organisations. XSL enables the manipulation of style sheets through scripting: as CSS1 and CSS2 describe how documents are presented, XSL enables 'user extensibility', that is a script for functions such as embedding a font can be written and attached to a style sheet. The benefit of XSL is that it will clearly separate content from presentation, potentially speeding up production of web sites as writers can write content without having to worry about the appearance of a page.

CGI

Probably the most useful extension to web sites is CGI (Common Gateway Interface), a protocol built into HTTP that enables web pages to transfer instructions to applications stored on a web server. These instructions are processed on the server and the results sent back as HTML, for example notification that email has been sent or a form received. By providing a standard interface, CGI enables developers to use a wide range of programming tools to provide interactivity and process data.

CGI programs are often referred to as scripts because the first applications were written using UNIX shell scripts, commands similar to DOS instructions but considerably more powerful. It is possible to use programs such as C to produce CGI applications, but one worth learning because it is relatively simple and widely supported is Perl (see below). It is also possible to use CGI scripts that are pre-written and can be adapted for your web site. Such scripts must be hosted on a web server in a CGI script folder, and most ISPs already have basic CGI scripts for counting page hits or processing forms.

To be useful, a CGI script must be executable: the browser calling it must not simply be able to read it but also run the program. Some ISPs allow users to run programs from any point within their web directory; others, because of security issues, insist on running files from one directory only, usually cgi-bin (for 'binaries'). Other ISPs, particularly free accounts, will not allow CGI access at all – because the program is executed on the server rather than the visitor's computer, CGI scripts can place a burden on the server.

CGI is usually integrated into an HTML document as part of a form, using the METHOD and ACTION attributes. These tell the browser how to send information back to the server and where the script is located. METHOD takes one of two forms, GET and POST: GET appends the information to the end of the URL and is limited to a total of 255 characters, including the ACTION URL, which can be a problem when collating information from a complicated form. POST, on the other hand, sends each value to the server and so has no character limitations.

For example, a common CGI line would appear as follows:

```
<FORM METHOD="POST" ACTION="/cgi-bin/myscript">
```

In the above example, each value from a form is posted in turn and the information processed by a script which could email values to the web developer or generate a page depending on the results posted from the form.

Server-side includes

Another type of interactivity comes from server-side includes (SSI, also known as server-parsed HTML, or SHTML). Like CGI, SSI runs on the server rather than in the browser and can be useful for improving the development of a site. At its simplest, SSI tends to be used to standardise pages, inserting a button bar for example on every page: updates to the bar can be made by changing one file rather than having to edit the entire site.

Such SSI commands are embedded in HTML comments, similar to JavaScript instructions, such as the following to include a link to a button console:

```
<!-#include virtual="console.html"->
```

This command inserts the code contained in the file console.html into the page where it appears.

As well as simplifying site development, the main use of SSI and CGI is to take information passed from the browser to the server and process it. This can be used to collect information from visitors, to direct them to particular pages on a site depending on particular requirements and, increasingly, to sell goods across the Internet.

Perl

Perl, which has been described as the 'Swiss Army penknife' of the web, stands for Practical Extraction and Reporting Language. Anyone seriously interested in producing fully functioning interactive web sites should spend time learning some of the basics of Perl: it is extremely powerful, is much easier than C to use – particularly as it lends itself so easily to customisation – and is present on just about every UNIX web server, as well as plenty of those running Windows NT or WebStar for the Mac.

Perl is an interpreted language, which means that code is not compiled for a particular platform but source code is converted to machine code on the fly each time the program runs. What this means is that Perl is slower than a language such as C, but it remains worth learning; on average, Perl is about 2.5 times slower than C but 10 times faster than Java. In particular, it can achieve tasks in one line of code that would required hundreds in any other. Only for sites expecting tens of thousands of hits per day will Perl be insufficient.

The language is bundled with most releases of UNIX or Linux, and versions are available for Windows from www.perl.org. The following is an example of a very simple Perl script:

```perl
#!usr/bin/perl
#Generate a page of HTML showing date and time on
the fly
print 'Content-type: text/html\n\n';
print '<HTML><HEAD><TITLE>Hello
world</TITLE></HEAD>\n';
print '<BODY><H1>Hello World</H1><br>\n';
# Display the date and time
print 'Date and time:', scalar localtime, '\n';
print '<BODY></HTML>\n';
```

There are several features to note about the above script. First of all, comments are indicated by the hash (#) mark, and the first line (beginning #!) is important to indicate where Perl is located on the server; when customising a script, this may need to be changed to the actual path provided by the ISP.

Generated output is indicated by the command print, with the first line indicating the content type. The characters \n may not be required, but are used to indicate a line return on a UNIX server, and two returns (\n\n) provide a clear space between the content type and the remaining HTML. Pre-formatted output is indicated by the material between quotation marks, while the information generated on the fly, the date and time, is indicated by the instruction 'scalar localtime'.

One of the advantages of using Perl is that there are several sites, such as www.worldwidemart.com, that supply royalty-free scripts that can be adapted for your own site. Rather than having to write a script from scratch, you can download these files and customise them for your new site; to simplify the task of customisation even more, many scripts place the information that needs to be changed as a series of variables near the beginning of the file.

ASP

Active Server Pages (ASP) is Microsoft's way of creating dynamic web pages as an extension to its Internet Information Services (IIS). A browser requesting an ASP page (indicated by the extension .asp instead of .htm) does not have the page returned directly; rather, it is parsed so that scripts are run on the server to insert new content, such as a database query, to the client.

Unlike scripting languages such as Perl, ASP is usually embedded within the HTML code for a page, and is indicated by the delimiters <% ... %>. To create an ASP page, all you need is a text editor to write the code before saving it with the extension .asp.

As well as server-side scripting to include information within pages, ASP can be used for routine tasks, such as storing data as a variable and tracking visitors as they navigate from page to page, both of which are useful for passing information between pages, say for e-commerce.

A sample page using ASP to determine different genres for a reader would look something like the following:

```
<% IF SESSION("username")="" then %>
<H2>Please tell us the type of book you like to
read</H2><P>
<FORM>
<INPUT TYPE="radio" NAME="genre"
VALUE="Crime">Crime<BR>
<INPUT TYPE="radio" NAME="genre"
VALUE="Historical">Historical<BR>
<INPUT TYPE="radio" NAME="genre" VALUE="SF">SF<BR>
<INPUT TYPE="radio" NAME="genre"
VALUE="Romance">Romance<BR>
<INPUT TYPE=Submit>
</FORM>
<%else%>
<H2><%= SESSION("username") %> - welcome to your
chosen genre</H2>
<% END IF %>
```

Java and ActiveX

Java was developed by programmers at Sun Microsystems as a user-interface programming language called Oak which was supposed to revolutionise the way that consumers interacted with electronic devices. In 1994 (no one having bought Oak), Sun began to adapt it for the Internet and, in 1995, renamed it Java.

Java is unusual in that it does not run directly within the operating system of the computer, but rather is operated from a software-driven 'virtual computer', or 'virtual machine'. The virtual machine is specific to the platform on which the browser is running, whether a PC running an operating system such as Windows, Linux, OS/2, a Mac or other computer such as a Silicon Graphics or Sun workstation. While this virtual computer is specific to the particular platform, however, the code that it implements is not, meaning that an applet can be written once and run across different computers without the need for recompiling.

If one of the golden rules of web design is speedy download times, loading a site with Java applets is a sure way to annoy users because most of them are not fast. That said, Java does offer certain sophisticated facilities, and the good news is that you do not need to be a programmer to use it. Programs such as Jamba and Director can output Java files but, for many of the most useful applets, you will need to use a programming tool such as Visual Café.

In addition, pre-made Java applications can be placed directly into web pages using applications such as Dreamweaver or Frontpage. Two of the best sites for Java applets are www.gamelan.com and the Sun site at java.sun.com.

Part of the excitement generated by Java was the fact that it did not rely on a particular operating system, which was particularly important to Microsoft competitors such as Sun. Microsoft responded in two ways. First of all, it 'improved' Java to execute more quickly on Windows machines. It also promoted its own alternative to straight Java: ActiveX.

ActiveX is a set of technologies that ties together different functions and programs to offer web producers more control over how information is presented on a page. It is not really a competitor to Java in the sense that it is not a programming language, but enables other components, such as Excel spreadsheets, to be displayed via a browser.

Microsoft released an ActiveX Control Pad to help web designers create and use ActiveX components, but these have also been extended beyond the web to other developments. The Control Pad includes a text editor, an object editor for placing ActiveX controls directly into a document, a set of controls and a Script Wizard for adding scripts to pages. It can be downloaded from msdn.microsoft.com/fnf.asp.

MULTIMEDIA

Audio-visual material can be entertaining and informative, but the web was originally designed for text and the occasional image. As such, it has not yet fully developed into a broadcast medium, and is still struggling with issues relating to bandwidth, the amount of information that can be transmitted across the telephone wires and satellites that constitute the Internet. Full screen, all-singing, all-dancing sound and video is out of the question, so use audio and video carefully.

Internet video also utilises streaming, a means of providing audio-visual materials as quickly as possible by playing sound and video as soon as it begins to arrive, rather than waiting for the entire file to download. Streaming divides files into smaller packets of images or sounds that can be displayed almost immediately. The main AV formats are:

MPEG   small and fast but, particularly with MPEG2, capable of providing high-quality video as used in DVD.

MP3 or MPEG3   another highly compressed format used for sound which provides up to CD quality in smaller files and also provides for streaming.

AVI   the Windows native format; capable of high-quality video but with large file sizes. AVI is not capable of streaming and is not supported on Macs.

WAV   sound-file format, used primarily by Windows; can provide high-quality, CD sound but, without compression, results in large file sizes.

AU/AIF   sound-file format similar to WAV, but native to the Mac.

RealVideo/RealAudio   popular formats on the web, and capable of providing fast, streaming sound and video. Quality is not particularly high, however.

QuickTime   another high-quality video format, and versions 3 and 4 also support streaming. Compression rates are higher with version 4.

Shockwave Audio   an audio format from Macromedia which is based on MP3 to compress WAV and AU/AIFF files.

The most important rule for audio and video is that small really is beautiful. As well as reducing the size of video frames, if you are going to use AV materials on your web site consider packages such as Adobe AfterEffects or Equilibrium's DeBabelizer, which reduce frame counts or colours to make files as small as possible without destroying them completely.

Real media

RealAudio, released by RealNetworks' in 1995, was something of a revolution at the time in terms of streaming data across the web, meaning that users no longer had to wait for long downloads before they could begin listening to files, opening the potential of online radio and music channels. With RealVideo, streaming video also began to take off and, while the quality of Real media has been overtaken in the form of

MPEG video and MP3 sound files, the RealSystem plug-in remains one of the most popular on the web.

The Real plug-in can handle high-quality audio as well as video, and also play other, non-Real format files such as AVI, WAV and even Flash. The plug-in actually consists of three parts: RealPlayer, RealProducer and RealServer. RealPlayer is used to download and play files produced with RealProducer software. Versions of these are available as free downloads, as is a limited version of RealServer, the web server software designed specifically to serve Real media using a proprietary protocol. While RealServer is no longer required to serve Real Media files, playback now being handled increasingly on the client (browser) side, the server is useful for webcasting, and offers multiple playback rates depending on the visitor's connection. Many ISPs now offer RealServer support.

The limited freeware version of RealServer (restricted to twenty-five simultaneous streams) is available from www.real.com, as are RealPlayer and RealProducer.

Flash and Shockwave

While most protocols for the web are devised through a range of manufacturers or the World Wide Web Consortium, there has also been a thriving industry in plug-ins, that is third-party software used to display files incorporated into web pages that do not use standard HTML. Among the most successful of these plug-ins are Flash and Shockwave, developed by the multimedia company Macromedia.

Macromedia bought the application Future Splash, a vector-based drawing and animation tool that could produce very small files for downloading, and successfully marketed it to become the most successful plug-in on the web. Flash has since moved on to become a tool with uses ranging from creating small animations and advertisement banners to complete interactive solutions.

Flash files are a subset of the Shockwave protocol, devised to enable web browsers to display interactive content produced within Macromedia's flagship product, Director. While preserving the interactive multimedia of Director files, Shockwave also compresses and streams files, that is, it plays those files as soon as they begin to download and also enables files to be linked, so that only sections that are required are downloaded.

In combination with JavaScript, Flash is probably the most effective way of providing web pages with attractive and compelling interactivity while maintaining fast download times. Since Macromedia acquired it, Flash has been steadily enhanced and compatibility extended – Macromedia claims that over 80 per cent of browsers are Flash compatible.

Director, from which Shockwave files are produced, uses film metaphors to organise key components, with 'casts' (incorporating anything from a sound or image file to scripts and navigation components) that are arranged on a 'stage' according to instructions from a 'score'. While a difficult program to use, Director remains one of the best multimedia tools around and is more important than ever as Macromedia has targeted it increasingly towards the web. For details on Flash and Director, as well as demos that can be downloaded, see www.macromedia.com.

4
Production: designing for the web

Web designers often rush in where angels fear to tread. We have spent a considerable amount of time on pre-production issues – selecting the appropriate tools, determining who and what a site is for, how it is to be developed – because it cannot be emphasised enough that time spent planning a web site will save hours further down the line.

Thus this book has outlined ways of thinking strategically about the web, why you may be considering building a site and the tools and technologies you will need to create and manage your pages. The next step is to take these tools and construct a compelling web site, and this chapter will take you through some basic procedures of web design before moving on to dynamic content in the next chapter.

Before launching into web design, however, there still remain some factors that should be thought through when planning a site, particularly how it will look and work, how visitors will navigate through the site and what images, colours and text you will use. This chapter will therefore cover some basic design principles before going on to demonstrate web design in basic and professional packages.

DESIGN PRINCIPLES

Design is frequently thought of in terms of the appearance of a site – its aesthetics, how it looks. While this is very valid, and appearance contributes greatly to the success or failure of a site, design is also a question of usability. Just as a chair may look great but be impossible to sit on for extended periods of time, or a car may blow away the competition in terms of its sleek lines but guzzle gas like the villain in a Mad Max movie, so a web site that appears serene and sublime on the surface may leave visitors fuming with suppressed rage at best, indifferent at worst, if they cannot find what they want.

This chapter therefore begins not with the use of colour, graphics and other design elements such as typography – important though they are – but rather with the navigation of a site, how the visitor is to move around it and, following the Bauhaus precept that form follows function, make use of its contents. Finally, bear in mind that visitors to your site may not be using the hardware and software you have used to design that site, at the very least that they may be using a different browser.

Navigation

A well-designed web site does not simply consist of an aesthetically pleasing interface, but is also easy to navigate: or rather, the means to creating an aesthetically pleasing interface include paying attention to navigation as well as to images and other design elements.

Good navigation depends on techniques for accessing the web site – interface design – as well as how the site looks. For example, users with slower connections may browse the web with images toggled off, so text-only alternatives are a necessity: these may consist of a separate list of links, or using the ALT tag to include a line of text alongside the image. In addition, visitors with disabilities may not be able to distinguish certain colours or use a mouse to navigate sites, requiring sites to be accessible via keystrokes. For more information on providing access for users with disabilities, see www.skill.org.uk.

Navigation tools should, ideally, be consistent in positioning and overall look and feel, as well as provide feedback to a visitor. If you change the position of a home page on each new page, browsers may become disoriented. Likewise, visually consistent navigation tools play an important part in constructing the image of your site. Regarding feedback, there are several simple and common techniques that are useful in providing information to users: it is common, for example, to include a greyed-out version of a particular graphic which is shown when a link is unavailable, such as when the link would simply take the user to the page already displayed; highlighting is also especially useful to indicate when a link can be followed, and this is probably the single most common usage of JavaScript on the web.

While the types of web site may vary considerably, many share some common features. First of all, most sites open with a home or front page:

like the contents page of a book, a good front page should provide some sort of overview of the different sections of a site, even if it is only links that enable visitors to see what is available: mapping your site is an important basic principle for successful navigation.

A common mistake when setting out these divisions is to lay out different sections in a radically distinct way, which can only serve to confuse visitors. A more successful technique is to implement the same basic design, with common buttons located in the same place, but change small elements of a page, for example a toolbar: this can help orient visitors within a site (they know that the page they are looking at is a news item rather than a review, for example), without perplexing them unnecessarily.

Some of the most common navigation devices that work on the web are as follows:

'Sidebars' and 'topbars'   These provide consistent designs across a site, are usually visible and yet still allow room for content. Many commercial sites use combinations of sidebars and topbars, providing a top-level view of content as well as more complex or specific links.

Frames   Overuse of frames can be extremely frustrating for visitors, particularly those using older browsers and smaller displays. Used well, however, frames can be particularly effective for navigation where a producer wishes to display a consistent, unchanging toolbar that is downloaded once and thus speeds up the general performance of the site. (See 'Working with frames' below.)

JavaScript and Java   JavaScript is particularly useful for providing simple feedback to visitors in the form of rollover buttons that change shape or colour when the mouse moves over them. More complex sites may use Java or ActiveX components to create directory 'tree' structures.

Text   Because images may not display as you intend, if at all, text alternatives are essential on a web site.

Some things to avoid when designing navigation for your site are:

Plug-ins   With the possible exception of Flash, using buttons that require a plug-in is generally a bad idea. If visitors need to download that plug-in even before they can move through your site, the chances are they will never return.

Floating navigation panels   While these may look very impressive at first glance, navigation tools that occupy their own window are easily lost behind other windows.

Java only   While Java may provide some useful tools for navigation, older browsers may not display them, so provide alternatives. Also, while the most common use for JavaScript is to create rollover buttons, remember that you need to set up scripts so that non-JavaScript compatible browsers will not choke on them.

Redundant links   Links to non-existent pages, as well as links to a page that the visitor is currently on, can be annoying.

Graphics

Images are inserted into a web page using the tag <IMG> and the attribute SRC, which indicates where the file is located in relation to the page. For example, <IMG SRC="images/boat.jpg"> indicates that the file boat.jpg is found in a directory called images.

Using graphics in web pages is often a compromise between appearance and download times: the best-looking site in the world is also likely to be the least visited if users have to spend too long downloading images. A realistic assumption is that most Internet users will be connected to the Internet with a modem capable of 3–4Kb per second, meaning that an optimistic download time for a typical 30Kb image is at least seven seconds. Overloading pages with too many graphics, or images with large file sizes, therefore, will deter visitors.

The primary rule for using web graphics is: compression, compression, compression. This is often a straight trade-off between file size and image quality, but using a specialised application such as Fireworks or ImageReady can make a significant difference by slicing complex graphics and compressing different sections at different rates. Also, bear in mind the virtues of the main graphic formats on the web:

JPEG   JPEG images make use of lossy compression (that is they discard information, flattening areas of similar colour into one colour) to compact an image as aggressively as possible. These are useful for full-colour images such as photos.

GIF   GIF images generally use lossless compression, whereby redundant colours are calculated by a mathematical formula. GIFs are restricted to 256 colours, and complex images such as photographs are usually larger as GIFs than as JPEGs; however, if you are creating images using large areas of simple colour, such as logos or buttons, GIFs can produce smaller file sizes and sharper, clearer images. GIFs can also be animated and display one colour as transparent.

PNG   Portable Network Graphics are a later generation of images that can preserve Photoshop-like layers, making them easy to work with, but combine some of the features of GIFs with high, JPEG style compression rates and colours. The fact that only new browsers can display these styles has resulted in their being adopted only slowly.

One way to optimise graphics is by 'image-slicing': when an image is compressed as a single graphic, the resultant file makes a compromise between the range of colours to be displayed and file sizes. Preserve crisp, sharp images with a wide range of colours and the file size will be too large; on the other hand, reduce file sizes too much and the image will appear muddy and blurred.

Image-slicing divides the image into several different areas based on the ranges of colours used in the graphic. Each of these slices can be reduced to the smallest possible size but, because colours are within a certain range for each slice, the image should appear much clearer. Editors which support image-slicing will also produce an HTML table for reassembling the picture which can be cut and pasted into another web page.

Another tip for optimising the speed of a page is to include the attributes HEIGHT and WIDTH (measured in pixels) for the IMG tag. If these attributes are not included, the browser has to calculate the dimensions of an image before displaying it: while for a single image this will not be noticeable, for a page with several images it is worthwhile including these dimensions, for example <IMG SRC="../images/history_title.gif' HEIGHT=50 WIDTH=150>, to speed up how the browser draws a page. To further aid navigation, also use the ALT attribute: this provides an alternative text description when the image is not displayed, for example, ALT="Link to history page".

BETTER BY DESIGN

There are plenty of new media agencies sprouting up, eager to show off their talents and also providing inspiration to aspiring web producers. Studio Soup (www.studiosoup.co.uk), for example, producers of the *Young Money* and Virgin Direct sites, offers a very clean and simple home site, while Monkey Media (www.monkey.com) demonstrates how to use Flash in an entertaining manner.

For URLs that offer a triumph of content as well as style, the beautiful BirdGuides site (www.birdguides.com) has won a BAFTA award two years in a row (Figure 4.1), while Falmouth's professional writing magazine, *Bloc* (www.falmouth.ac.uk/bloc/) was awarded a *Guardian* student prize in 1999. For lessons in usability and navigation, as well as how to offer services to potential customers, visit the Lufthansa site (www.lufthansa.de), which was recently nominated the best business site by Novell in its yearly Worldwide Web 100.

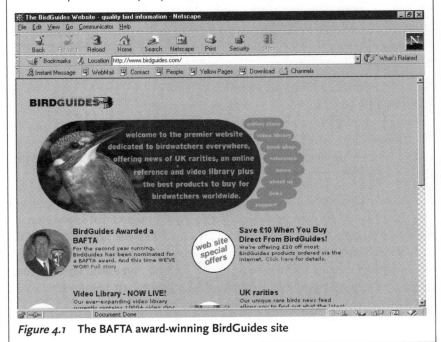

Figure 4.1   **The BAFTA award-winning BirdGuides site**

Working with colour

Simple but dramatic graphical effects are often achieved not by employing complex graphics but by the accomplished use of colour. Many colours are said to be complementary – for example yellow and black or blue and yellow, and a rather bland page can be improved dramatically by placing a colour logo or small graphic in a noticeable position. By contrast, using too many different colours, or colours that clash, usually makes a page look tawdry and difficult to use. Also, bear in mind that colour-blind visitors may have a problem distinguishing certain colours, such as red and green.

When creating graphics and using colour in web pages, it is often important to bear in mind the so-called 'web-safe palette', which consists of 216 colours. If you have any experience at all of designing for print, this range of rather garish colours will probably strike you with horror. Nonetheless, just as you have to take into account the fact that JavaScript and HTML tags may be incompatible with different browsers, so colours can vary from browser to browser.

While the very old computers capable of displaying no more than 16 colours are *unlikely* to be connected to the web, a substantial number of visitors to a site may be using a machine capable of displaying no more than 256 colours. Although the computer you design on may display millions of colours, someone using such a display may see your beautifully designed graphics as an ugly shade of grey.

Some graphics applications save to a 'web-safe' colour palette, which consists of 216 colours. The reason this is only 216 rather than 256 colours is that there are inconsistencies between the colours on Mac- or Windows-based systems: of the colours used by each operating system, only 216 overlap and are safe to use. Using any of these colours means that your images will display as intended on either system.

For computers displaying only 256 colours, images using colours outside this palette can be displayed in two ways: dithered (whereby two or more colours are mixed in a pattern, say white and red to create pink) or by converting a colour to the nearest shade within that palette. What this means is that, if you wish your graphics and colours to be viewed by as many people as possible, you should change your display settings to 256 colours to test your pages.

Colour crunching

Every colour is defined as a combination of red, green and blue values (RGB), and the number of colours that a system can display on screen is determined by the number of bits that it can support. Each spot of colour has one pixel each for red, green and blue, and the shade of the colour ranges from 0 (no colour) to 255 (the maximum amount of that colour). Thus black (no light and therefore no colour for that pixel) is 0 for each RGB value, while white is 255.

Many web and image editors represent colours as hexadecimals using two numbers from 0 to 9 or two letters from A to F (that is 10 to 15) to represent each RGB value. Thus black is 000000, while white is FFFFFF, unmixed red FF0000 and yellow mixing red and green FFFF00.

Regarding the number of colours that can be displayed, or the colour depth, increasing the amount of information in the form of bits increases the range of colour exponentially. The smallest colour range is on or off, black or white, and is referred to as one-bit colour. More common are 8-bit colour displays, providing 256 colours, or 24-bit colour with over 16 million hues.

DESIGN TIPS

- **Three golden rules for Internet design:** Clarity, interactivity and download times. The most exciting and attractive site in the world will become a lot less interesting and attractive if users have to wait half an hour for pages to download. Visitors want a site that is a pleasure to use, simple to navigate through and loads quickly in their browsers.

- **Always consider your audience:** Bear in mind that most people do not have a 19', or even a 17', monitor capable of displaying 1024 × 768 resolutions or higher, running the latest browser on the fastest PIII or G4 with a leased line.

- **Make your navigation controls consistent:** Create a template design and then stick to it, so that visitors aren't confused as they move between pages. You may need different buttons on each page, but try and locate links in the same place.

- **Less is more:** Don't overload your page with fonts, graphics and animations:

not only can these take longer to download, too many cause your site to appear messy.

- **Frontload important material:** Visitors tend to work through web pages very quickly unless something grabs their attention. Consequently you should place important material near the beginning.

- **Evaluate new technologies:** Just because something is available on the web does not mean that it is automatically worth placing on your site. Test new ideas and technologies before using them on your site.

CREATING A SITE: BASIC FEATURES

Using Netscape Composer

Having covered some general principles of planning, design and navigation, it is time to create a web site. We'll begin with a very basic site that includes formatted text, links and images using a commonly used web editor, Netscape Composer. The virtues of this application are that it is free with Communicator, available on a wide range of platforms, and offers a number of tools to provide relatively sophisticated web pages.

The site to be created on the following pages is a brief guide to Cornwall, its history, places to go and where to stay. Images and text for this site can be found on the *Producing for the Web* site at www.producing.routledge.com/resources.htm. To compare your work to the finished site, go to www.producing.routledge.com/kernow/default.html.

Before designing a home page, the first task is to set a root directory, a folder where pages will be stored. It is typical to place the home page here, along with one or two top-level pages, but with other web pages and images stored in folders that will make the site easier to organise and manage. Within this directory create two more folders, one called images and the other called pages: all documents other than the home page will be placed in either of these two folders. When you have created the images folder, download the images for this tutorial from the *Producing for the Web* site and store them, or copies of them, here.

Once our root directory is created, the next task is to make our home page. Composer is divided into three main parts: at the top of the screen are the menu bar, composition toolbar and formatting toolbar (if you cannot see the last two, go to View, Show in the menu bar and click each one); beneath this is the workspace where the components of a page are arranged; at the bottom of the page is the status bar, showing information about the page and containing the component bar from which users can access other parts of Communicator.

Working with text, colour and images

Our home page will consist of a single image and a series of links leading to other parts of the site. First of all, we will change the colour of our page: the default for Composer is white, which will be fine for pages with a lot of text but, for this page, change the colour to green. To customise the colours on a page, go to Format, Page Colors and Properties, which shows the Page Properties dialog box. There are three tabs at the top of this box: General, Colors and Background, and META Tags. Meta tags will be dealt with in chapter six, and most of the information in the General screen can be ignored, but next to the heading Title enter 'Kernow Home Page'.

Clicking on the Colors and Background tab shows the options for changing text and background colours. Clicking each of the buttons in the Page Colors section allows users to change background, text and link defaults: a box appears with 'web-safe' colours, but clicking on Other allows designers to set one of 16 million colours.

As you move your mouse over each of the web-safe colours, a hexadecimal number is displayed. Select the dark green with the value R=0, G=153, B=0 for the background colour. For the link colour, select the lightest green (R=153, G=255, B=153) and then click OK. It is now time to save our page: go to File, Save and, in the root directory, give the document the title home.html. If you have not already provided a title, Composer will prompt you as it saves the page.

Having set our basic colours, we now wish to add an image. Press return and click the Image button, or go to Insert, Image. This displays the Image Properties box, which again has three tabs, for formatting links, paragraphs and images. Beneath the images tab are options to change how text wraps around an image, its size and, at the top, the address of the image. Assuming that you have saved it into the images folder, click on Choose File and then navigate to that folder and select the file cross.gif. Ensure that 'Leave image at original location' is checked (to prevent Composer making a copy of it into the root directory) and click OK for it to appear on the page. Select the image by clicking on it and then, in the formatting toolbar, select Center from the Alignment button or go to Format, Align, Center. This places the image in the middle of the page.

We have almost finished our first page, but we now need to add the text for our links. Press return twice and then enter the following text, pressing tab between each item: History, Places, Where to stay, Secret Cornwall and Search. As you enter this text, it should be centred on the page; if it is not, align it as you did the image, then select the text with the mouse and make it bold by clicking on the bold A in the formatting toolbar or going to Format, Style, Bold. Your page should appear as in Figure 4.2.

Using tables

We are now ready to create our second page, which will be linked to the home page and also form a template for other pages. To make a slightly

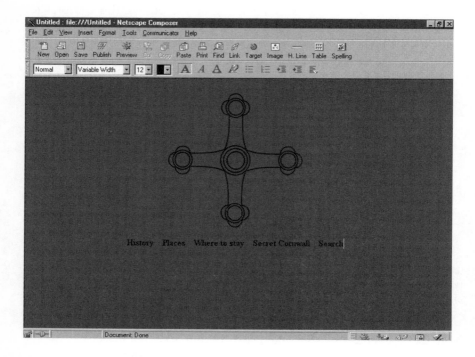

Figure 4.2   **The Kernow home page**

more sophisticated design, we will also use tables to organise images, text and links.

Click on the New button in Composer, or go to File, New, and select Blank Page, which will open a separate window. The first thing we wish to do is set the colour for links and insert a background image. Save the page as template.html in the directory pages and go to Format, Page Colors and Properties and change the Link Text colour to the same colour we used for our home page's background (R=0, G=153, B=0), which will show up more clearly against our light background. For the background image, click Use Image and select backgrnd.gif from the folder images; ensure that 'Leave image at original location' is checked and then select OK.

Now, add a title to your page: click on the Insert Image button and select the image history_title.gif, then align it in the centre of the page. To insert the table, move the cursor to the right of the title and click the Insert Table button or go to Insert, Table, to display the New Table Properties box. More advanced editors such as Dreamweaver use layers to emulate DTP applications, but HTML 3.2 editors such as Composer require tables. While these may seem complex at first, they can be used very effectively to lay out components (the default for HTML being to run text and images from top to bottom), and indeed even the most advanced editors can save layers as tables for the sake of backwards compatibility.

A table forms a grid in which text, images, links and other components are stored. Because each cell can be formatted individually, elements of a page can be aligned and arranged without changing the overall structure of a page. In addition, tables can be nested inside other tables, creating extremely complex pages.

For our template, we wish to create a simple table that is two columns wide and two rows high. Under the heading Table Alignment, select Center, and set the Border line width to 0; by default, tables appear with a visible border around them, but to use them as place holders this should be invisible. Leave Cell Padding as 1, but change Cell Spacing to 5. Cell spacing is the number of pixels between each cell while padding is the number of pixels between the cell border and its contents. Next, change the Table Width to 620 pixels and make sure that Equal Column Widths is not selected. Setting a resolution to less than 640 will ensure that the page displays on even the smallest monitor, and the contents of the table will be centred with a white margin on larger screens.

The next stage is to change the dimensions of individual cells. Right-click in the top left hand cell and select Table Properties. This displays a dialog box similar to the New Table box, but with three tabs, for Table, Row and Cell. Click the Cell tab and change the Vertical Alignment to Top (the default is to place elements in the middle of the cell) and change the Cell Width to 100 pixels and set the Cell Span to 2 rows. When you click OK, the cell will appear much larger than the others and now spans two rows, with a third column having been added. Right-click in this new cell and select Delete, Cell, or place the cursor within it and go to Edit, Delete Table, Cell. Finally, right-click in the two remaining right-hand cells, select Table Properties and, under Cell, set the vertical alignment for each to Top and set their width at 520 pixels.

Understanding tables

Creating a table by hand is a laborious task but the importance of tables as a layout tool cannot be overemphasised. Even if you are using a sophisticated web editor with layers to drag and drop elements onto a page, for widespread compatibility with older browsers you will still need to save your design as a table.

Tables are contained between the <TABLE> ... </TABLE> tags, these being used with several attributes including WIDTH (defined in terms of pixels or percentage of the window), ALIGN, BORDER, CELLSPACE and CELLPADDING. A table is a grid consisting of rows and columns defined by the <TR> ... </TR> and <TD> ... </TD> tags. The <TD> or table data tag is used to define cells, and the number of cells in a row will determine how many columns the table has.

The table data tag is very versatile, and uses a number of parameters to define each cell's attributes. Cells may span one or more columns or rows using COLSPAN and ROWSPAN, may have their contents aligned horizontally or vertically using ALIGN and VALIGN, and may be formatted with different background colours and images.

A basic table would look as follows:

```
<TABLE>
    <TR>
            <TD>Row 1, Column 1</TD>
            <TD>Row 1, Column 2</TD>
    </TR>
    <TR>
            <TD>Row 2, Column 1</TD>
            <TD>Row 2, Column 2</TD>
    </TR>
</TABLE>
```

Setting links

We have now nearly completed our template. Move the cursor to beneath the table and press return, then type in the following text, again pressing tab between each item: Home, History, Places, Where to stay, Secret Cornwall and Search. Make sure that the text is centred and bold, then click save.

The next step is to create links. Highlight Home and click on the Insert Links button, or go to Insert, Link to display the Character Properties dialog box. Links are indicated in HTML by use of the anchor tag <A> … </A> surrounding the text or image which is the hot spot that users can click on to move between pages. The first anchor uses the attribute HREF (hypertext reference) to indicate the address of its target, for example:

```
<A HREF="http://www.yahoo.com">Click here to visit
Yahoo!</A>
```

Links may be either absolute or relative. An absolute link, as in the above example, is an address to a specific site on a server that must include all path information to that file, such as http://www.myisp.com/-mypage.html, and is useful for creating links to external web sites. A relative link, on the other hand, is defined in relation to the current page. Thus the link to our title image is ../images/history_title.gif, that is history_title.gif is located in the directory called images. Directories and their contents are indicated by a forward slash, and to refer to a directory above the current one you must use two full stops.

It is best to use relative links for connecting to other pages on your site: if the directory in which all your pages on is moved, say to another ISP, the links will continue to work without any need for modification. For Home, click on Choose File and navigate to the root directory where you can select home.html. For the other links on this page, click the link button and type in the following addresses:

History   history.html

Places   places.html

Where to Stay   where.html

Secret Cornwall   secret.html

Search   search.html

As we add pages to our site in the folder pages, these links will appear on every page and provide a quick link to the top level of the site. Save your template, which should look like Figure 4.3.

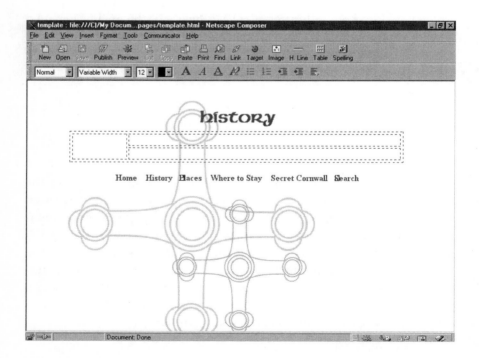

Figure 4.3   Template for the Kernow web site

Using the template

Now that our template is finished, we can use it to create our first page. In the folder pages, make a copy of template.html and rename it history.html before opening it in Composer. To add content to the pages, make sure the cursor is in the top right-hand cell and click on the image button; assuming that you have copied the file maentol.jpg to your images folder, select this image and click OK. Next, open the file history1a.txt and copy the text beside the image.

We now need to format the contents of this cell. First of all Select the line 'Cornwall: prehistory to millennium' and in the formatting toolbar change its format from Normal to Heading 3. If you save and preview your page, the text will begin by running at the bottom of the image and continuing underneath it, but it should run down the left-hand side. To do this, double-click on the image maentol.jpg and in the Image Properties dialog box select the button that shows text flowing around an image to the left. Also, rather than have text flush against the image, to create space around the picture set the 'Space around image' box to 5 pixels for each side.

When you click on OK, there will appear to be no change, but save your work and preview the page in the browser: the image should now be on the right hand of the cell with text running alongside. For the cell beneath this, use the picture boats1.jpg and copy the text history1b.txt, but this time set the text to run alongside the right hand side of the image. Finally, select the text in both cells and reduce its size from 12 (the default) to 10 points.

We now need to add links for pages that we will create dealing with the history of Cornwall after this introductory page. In the narrow, left-hand column, type in the following items using bold text, hitting return twice between each one: Prehistoric Cornwall, Medieval Cornwall, Industrial Cornwall and Modern Cornwall. Select each one in turn and enter the following file names as links: prehistoric.html, medieval.html, industrial.html and modern.html.

Save your work and open the home page in Composer: select the text "History", click on the Link button and choose the file history.html from the directory pages. When you preview your file in a web browser, you will now be able to move backwards and forwards between the Home and History pages.

We now need to create the history subsection of our site: copy history.html four times and rename the copies as prehistoric.html, medieval.html, industrial.html and modern.html. Text can be changed by cutting and pasting over the previous entries, while replacement images are selected by double clicking on the picture and selecting a new file. Use the following files to change each page:

prehistoric.html   prehistoric_title.gif/stone1.jpg/stone2.jpg
                         history2a.txt/history2b.txt

medieval.html   medieval_title.gif/church1.jpg/church2.jpg
                         history3a.txt/history3b.txt

industrial.html   industrial_title.gif/mine1.jpg/mine2.jpg
                         history4a.txt/history4b.txt

modern.html   modern_title.gif/beach1.jpg/beach2.jpg
                         history5a.txt/history5b.txt

To complete the History page, open it again in Composer and select the link to History at the bottom of the page and delete it: it could be confusing to visitors navigating around your site. We did not remove it before copying our other pages, however, as visitors to a page on industrial history, for example, may wish to return back to the top-level history page.

CREATING A SITE: INTERMEDIATE FEATURES

Creating image maps

The next page to add to the site is an image map. Image maps provide an additional means of linking documents: as links can be attached to text and images so an image map defines a set of areas on a picture, each of which can be linked to a different URL. There are two main methods of creating image maps: the original image map which was devised for HTML 2.0 and is more usually referred to as a server-side image map, and the HTML 3.2, or client-side, version.

Server-side image maps are supported by just about any browser that can display images, but, as this involves configuring a CGI script, are used much less frequently than client-side maps. Although it is impossible to guarantee that all browsers visiting a site will be able to use a client-side map, the percentage of browsers incompatible with HTML 3.2 is negligible.

A map file is a series of (x,y) co-ordinates specifying the upper-left and lower-right areas of the defined areas of an image, with links to other pages. As with any HTML reference, it is possible to hand-code these co-ordinates, but creating an accurate image map can be incredibly difficult. Composer does not offer image map tools, but there are several shareware and freeware tools on the web, one that is particularly easy to use being Mapedit (www.boutell.com/mapedit/).

Before using Mapedit, from the file template.html create another file called places.html in Composer. Delete the table and the link to places, and insert the files places_title.jpg and map.jpg into the centre of the page. Save the file and then open Mapedit: a dialog box appears, asking which html file is to be opened (places.html) and which image is to be used to create a map (map.jpg). This image is then displayed, on which can be drawn a series of rectangles, ellipses or irregular shapes to define different areas as in Figure 4.4. As each area is drawn, another dialogue box appears, in which the linking URL and any alternative text or titles are entered. Draw a rectangle around each star and piece of text on the map and enter the following links for the four areas you define: tintagel.html, bodmin.html, falmouth.html, michael.html.

To create the pages for this section of the site, again use history.html as a template, renaming the copies as tintagel.html, bodmin.html, falmouth.html and michael.html. Change the links on the left-hand side of the page to the above URLs and substitute the following text and image files:

tintagel.html	tintagel_title.gif/tintagel1.jpg/tintagel2.jpg tintagel1.txt/tintagel2.txt
bodmin.html	bodmin_title.gif/bodmin1.jpg/bodmin.jpg bodmin1.txt/bodmin2.txt
falmouth.html	falmouth_title.gif/falmouth1.jpg/falmouth2.jpg falmouth1.txt/falmouth2.txt
michael.html	michael_title.gif/michael1.jpg/michael2.jpg michael1.txt/michael2.txt

Opening places.html in a text editor will reveal the code added by

Mapedit, which should look something like the following (the actual co-ordinates will vary):

```
<MAP NAME="map">
<AREA SHAPE="rect" COORDS="256,78,348,132"
HREF="tintagel.html">
<AREA SHAPE="rect" COORDS="301,160,398,214"
HREF="bodmin.html">
<AREA SHAPE="rect" COORDS="166,272,256,322"
HREF="falmouth.html">
<AREA SHAPE="rect" COORDS="68,300,154,366"
HREF="michael.html">
</MAP>
```

Working with frames

As well as displaying single pages, HTML 3.2 compatible browsers and above can display frames, that is, a single screen can be divided into a number of areas so that a sidebar or header displays links to pages.

Frames divide the browser's display window into several areas, each one displaying its own HTML document. By default, these documents operate independently of the others, so that a link in one frame will load

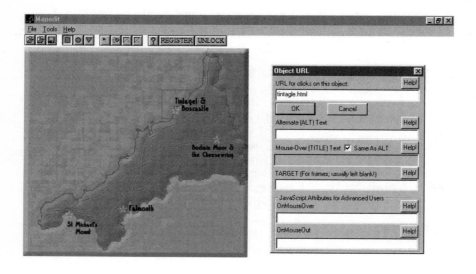

Figure 4.4   Creating an image map with MapEdit

other pages into that frame, but it is possible to load documents into different frames, so that a contents bar down the left-hand side, for example, will display linked pages in the main window on the right.

The basic step for dividing a browser into frames requires the use of a <FRAMESET> ... </FRAMESET> tag, which tells the browser to split the page vertically or horizontally into columns or rows. The FRAME-SET is kept in a separate document which loads other pages into the browser, for example:

```
<HTML>
<FRAMESET COLS="165,*">
<FRAME SRC="menu.htm" NAME="menu">
<FRAME SRC="body.htm" NAME="body">
<NOFRAMES>
<P>This web browser does not support frames.</P>
</NOFRAMES>
</FRAMESET>
</HTML>
```

The above code divides the page into two columns, the first on the left 165 pixels wide, the second on the right taking up the rest of the page (indicated by the asterisk). Into the left-hand side of the browser is loaded the page menu.htm, indicated by the SRC= attribute and given the name "menu", and on the right-hand side is loaded body.htm, given the name "body". The tag <NOFRAMES> provides a basic HTML page that is to be displayed if the browser does not support frames, displaying the text between the <P> ... </P> tags. It would also be possible to include a completely different design here or, more commonly, a link to another page that does not use frames.

If the page was to be divided horizontally rather than vertically, the attribute ROWS would be used after FRAMESET rather than COLS. Loading the page above displays the HTML documents with a distinct grey border between each frame. While there is nothing intrinsically wrong with using these borders, they can look very ugly, and so it is more usual to use the BORDER=0 attribute to remove such lines from the page. This provides a region for an image or banner at the top of the page, and a menu bar down the left-hand side.

In addition to setting border sizes, the FRAME tag uses the SCROLLING attribute to determine whether that panel scrolls or not (set to no, yes or auto depending on whether visitors can never scroll through a frame, must always scroll through it or will have a scroll bar appear depending on the size of the browser window) and sometimes the NORESIZE attribute, which indicates that a frame's size cannot be changed. Hence a frameset HTML with these attributes and three frames would look like this:

```
<FRAMESET BORDER=0 COLS="165,*">
<FRAME SRC="menu.htm" NORESIZE SCROLLING="no"
NAME="menu">
<FRAMESET BORDER=0 ROWS="100,*">
<FRAME SRC="head.htm" NORESIZE SCROLLING="no"
NAME="head">
<FRAME SRC="body.htm" NORESIZE SCROLLING="auto"
NAME="body">
</FRAMESET>
```

In the above HTML, the reason for ascribing names to different frames using the NAME attribute is to enable interframe links: for a menu with a number of buttons, creating a link which loaded a page into the menu frame would remove the means of navigating around the site and look dreadful. Using the TARGET attribute, however, links can be made to load in a specific frame as long as it is named: thus a link on the page menu.htm would look something like the following:

```
<A HREF="page1.htm" TARGET="body">
```

When creating a link to a page outside the site that is being worked on, TARGET="_top" should be used, to load the page in the main browser window rather than a subsidiary frame.

WHEN TO USE FRAMES

Frames are most commonly used to create side- or topbar menus for navigation around areas of a site. It is important, however, in many cases to retain backwards compatibility with browsers that are not compatible with frames.

If accessibility is paramount, then it may be necessary to create a site without frames. However, it is also possible to update an existing site very quickly to display content with or without frames. First of all, take the main home page of the site (such as default.htm, index.htm or something similar) and rename it something like mainpage.htm. Create a frameset reference page that is then given the original name of the former home page – this will enable existing bookmarks to locate a site. Then, in the area of HTML between <NOFRAMES> and </NOFRAMES> copy and paste the source code of your original home page: if the browser cannot use frames, it will simply display the single main page. If navigation links are included here as well as in a menu bar, users will be able to use the site without ever knowing the difference.

Alternatively, a new version of the index page could be created, without frames, that enables visitors to view the frame with frames or not (it may be, for example, that visitors with frame-compatible browsers would prefer to view a site without frames loading). Bear in mind also that visitors directed to your site from a search engine will probably load the page without frames.

Adding frames to our site

Before adding frames to the Kernow site, using the page home.html, we need to design the header that will appear above the home page. In Composer, create a new page and set its background colour to the same green as the home page, R=0, G=153, B=0. Save the file in the root directory next to home.html with the name header.

Next, define a table one row deep by six columns wide, aligned in the centre of the page with the border set to zero, width 600 pixels and columns equal width. When the table appears at the top of the new page, in each of the columns place the following pictures: home_button.gif, history_button.gif, places_button.gif, where_button.gif, secret_button.gif and search_button.gif.

Click on each of the images in turn and select the Link tab from the Image Properties dialog box. Choose files that go with each image – home.html, history.html, places.html, where.html, secret.html and search.html – and then click the button Extra HTML. In the window that appears, enter the text TARGET="body": when we create our frames, the larger area will be called body and all pages will be loaded into that frame rather than the header frame. After a link is added to an image, Composer tends to add a border around the image, so under the Image tab in Image Properties ensure that Solid border (in 'Space around image') is set to 0.

To create the frameset, open a text editor such as Notepad or SimpleText and enter the following:

```
<HTML>
<HEAD>
<TITLE>The Kernow web site
</TITLE>
</HEAD>
<FRAMESET BORDER=0 ROWS="80,*">
    <FRAME SRC="header.html" NORESIZE
SCROLLING="no" NAME="head">
    <FRAME SRC="home.html" NORESIZE
SCROLLING="auto" NAME="body">
</FRAMESET>
<NOFRAMES>
<HTML>
    <HEAD>
        <TITLE>Kernow home page</TITLE>
    </HEAD>
    <BODY TEXT="#000000" BGCOLOR="#009900"
LINK="#99FF99" VLINK="#551A8B" ALINK="#FF0000">
        <CENTER>
        <P><IMG SRC="images/cross.gif" height=251
width=250>
        <P><B><A HREF="pages/history.html">History
        </A>
        <A HREF="pages/places.html">Places</A>
        <A HREF ="pages/where.html">Where to
        stay</A>
        <A HREF ="pages/secret.html">Secret
        Cornwall</A>
        <A HREF="pages/search.html">Search</A></B>
        </CENTER>
    </BODY>
</HTML>
</NOFRAMES>
</FRAMESET>
</HTML>
```

Save the file as default.html. When you open this file, home.html and header.html will be loaded into the body and head frames respectively as in Figure 4.5. Clicking on each file will load the relevant page into the body frame, and the code between <FRAMES> and </NOFRAMES> will load the equivalent page to home.html even if the browser does not support frames. This ensures that the home page can be viewed by as many people as possible.

Writing basic JavaScript

Scripting is one way to make sites more dynamic, animating pages or components on pages, showing message boxes and collecting information to display different pages. JavaScript is a relatively simple scripting language compared to full-blown programming languages such as C or Pascal, but it is still complex compared to HTML, with manuals and books devoted to teaching its ins and outs. In this chapter, we will concentrate on one specific example of how JavaScript works to create a rollover button for our site.

Using the hyperlink tag <A>, JavaScript can trap key mouse movements to trigger events, typically loading a new page or activating a

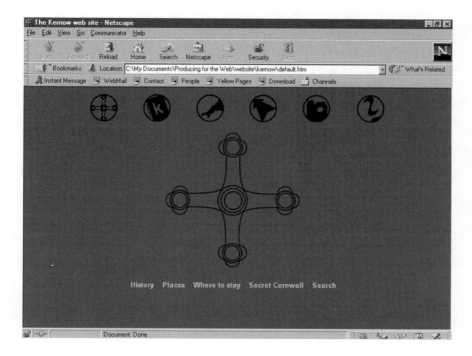

Figure 4.5   **The home page displayed with frames**

rollover button. The sequence of mouse events is as follows (for PC users, only the left mouse button is supported by these instructions):

Event	Meaning
onMouseOver	Mouse pointer moved over object
onMouseDown	Mouse button pressed
onMouseUp	Mouse button released
onMouseOut	Mouse pointer moved away from object

Creating rollover images

One of the simplest ways of providing feedback to a visitor is to create a rollover image, which works by substituting one image, whether a JPEG or GIF, with another. Such buttons can be made to work with most 3.0-plus browsers using JavaScript: when the mouse moves over the image, the replacement is substituted, when it moves out, the original image returns into position.

A basic script would run as follows:

```
<HTML>
<HEAD>
<TITLE>A simple script</TITLE>
    <SCRIPT LANGUAGE="JavaScript">
    <!--
    {flashout = new Image();
    flashout.src = "flash.gif";
    flashover = new Image();
    flashover.src = "flashover.gif"};
    function PicChange(ImageName,NewImage)
    {document.images[ImageName].src
    = eval(NewImage + ".src")}
    //-->
    </SCRIPT>
</HEAD>
<BODY>
    <A HREF="MyPage.htm"
onMouseOver="PicChange('flash','flashover')"
onMouseOut="PicChange('flash','flashout')">
    <IMG SRC="flash.gif" BORDER="0"
```

```
NAME="flash"></A>
</BODY>
</HTML>
```

The above script is divided into two parts: the header outlines the parameters of the script, identifying the script, providing a name ('flashout' and 'flashover') for the images and identifying their source ('flash.gif' and 'flashover.gif'): these names and the file names can be changed as required, but the rest of the script at this point should be copied as it appears above. PicChange is the JavaScript function, which is called in the second part of the script contained in the body of the page. To complete this part of the script, it is surrounded by <SCRIPT> and </SCRIPT> tags.

A rollover button must be attached to an anchor, though it is possible, as in this example, to link the page to itself so that nothing happens when a visitor clicks on it; more usually, a rollover button is used to highlight a link that does do something. The next part identifies the two JavaScript instructions – onMouseOver and onMouseOut – each of which swaps the current image (flash) for another (either flashover or flashout).

Next, the image source is identified and given a name: even though the image source is the same as the tag identified in the first part of the script, another name must be given for the image as it appears on the screen. This is a variable that can be substituted with another image source. If the NAME attribute is not included, the script will not work.

Adding rollover images to our site

To complete the default page for our Kernow site, the next step is to substitute rollover buttons in the header frame. Open the file header.html in a text editor; the first step is to define our variables, the six buttons which will be replaced by rollover images. To do this, enter the following code between the <HEAD> and </HEAD> tags (assuming that your images are stored in a folder called images):

```
<SCRIPT LANGUAGE="JavaScript">
   <!-- Hide script from incompatible browsers
   {homeout = new Image();
   homeout.src = "images/home_button.gif";
   homeover = new Image();
```

```
    homeover.src = "images/home_button_roll.gif";
    historyout = new Image();
    historyout.src = "images/history_button.gif";
    historyover = new Image();
    historyover.src =
"images/history_button_roll.gif";
    placesout = new Image();
    placesout.src = "images/places_button.gif";
    placesover = new Image();
    placesover.src =
"images/places_button_roll.gif";
    whereout = new Image();
    whereout.src = "images/where_button.gif";
    whereover = new Image();
    whereover.src = "images/where_button_roll.gif";
    secretout = new Image();
    secretout.src = "images/secret_button.gif";
    secretover = new Image();
    secretover.src =
"images/secret_button_roll.gif";
    searchout = new Image();
    searchout.src = "images/search_button.gif";
    searchover = new Image();
    searchover.src =
"images/search_button_roll.gif"};
    function PicChange(ImageName,NewImage)
    {document.images[ImageName].src
    = eval(NewImage + ".src")}
    //-->
</SCRIPT>
```

Having set these variables, the next step is to set the events that will trigger rollover images, the mouse over and mouse out events. The code for the table with images in should be amended to appear as follows:

```
<CENTER><TABLE BORDER=0 COLS=6 WIDTH="600" >
<TR>
<TD>
<CENTER><A HREF="home.html"
onMouseOver="PicChange('home','homeover')"
onMouseOut="PicChange('home','homeout')"
```

```
TARGET="body"><IMG SRC="images/home_button.gif"
NAME="home" BORDER=0 HEIGHT=55 WIDTH=55></A></CEN-
TER>
</TD>
```

Copy this code for each image, changing it so that links and PicChange references, as well as names, are amended accordingly, for example:

```
<TD>
<CENTER><A HREF="pages/history.html"
onMouseOver="PicChange('history','historyover')"
onMouseOut="PicChange('history','historyout')"
TARGET="body"><IMG SRC="images/history_button.gif"
NAME="history" BORDER=0 HEIGHT=55
WIDTH=55></A></CENTER>
</TD>
```

The other buttons should be changed to the following for links, name and rollover/rollout tags:

places_button.gif	places.html/places, placesover, placesout
where_button.gif	where.html/where, whereover, whereout
secret_button.gif	secret.html/secret, secretover, secretout
search_button.gif	search.html/search, searchover, searchout

This code is considerably more complex than the Flash rollover button. Whereas that was one button which could be repeated across a page, the header for the Kernow web site has six different rollover buttons indicating each part of the web site. Nonetheless, the principle is essentially the same for each button: the image has to be named as do the replacement images for the key events onMouseOver and onMouseOut. When you save the file and load it into a browser, the buttons at the top of the page will change as the mouse moves over them.

USING A PROFESSIONAL APPLICATION

Thus far we have created a home page and two main sections of our site, covering the basics of adding images, text and links to pages as well as using tables, frames and basic dynamic elements in the form of rollover buttons. The next chapter will demonstrate how to add more dynamic elements, but before then this chapter will conclude with an overview of a popular, cross-platform professional package, Dreamweaver.

Creating a site with Dreamweaver

Dreamweaver is one of the most sophisticated web editors available, and one which, at the time of writing, seems to be the closest for a standard application for web design. With Dreamweaver, currently at version 3, editors and designers have a multitude of tools for adding multimedia and dynamic effects to pages, as well as tools for managing a site.

We will recreate our basic web site using Dreamweaver, the interface of which is shown in Figure 4.6, as well as demonstrate some advanced features which are not available with an HTML 3.2 editor such as Composer.

Setting the site

The first step before creating our site is to define the root folder. Upon opening Dreamweaver, you will see three floating palettes, one for Objects, such as images and buttons, another for Properties, which

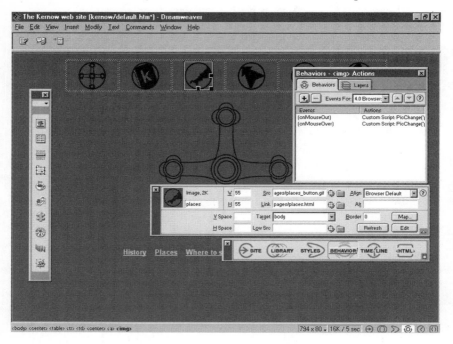

Figure 4.6 **Dreamweaver uses a visual interface for page design**

change as different components are selected on the page, and a Launcher palette. The last palette opens applications within Dreamweaver such as style and library inspectors, an HTML editor and, by clicking on the Site button, a site manager.

After entering the site manager, go to Site, New Site and set the root directory for your web site, then create two folders for images and pages. Copy the images downloaded from the *Producing for the Web* site into the former folder. The site manager is split into two screens, one for the site on a local machine, the other for the site on a remote server. Once a root location has been set, all pages and files will be saved in relation to this folder.

Creating pages

Dreamweaver enables designers to position content anywhere on the page by using layers, which function in a manner similar to frames and boxes in a DTP package such as Quark XPress. To use layers in the main editor, go to Modify, Layout, Reposition Content Using Layers. This will bring up a dialog box with four options: prevent layer overlap, show layer palette, show grid and snap to grid. The last two are relatively unimportant other than as aids to designing pages, while the layer palette enables users to select different layers more easily.

Preventing layers from overlapping, however, has important implications for page design. Browsers such as Internet Explorer 4 and Communicator 4 and above can display layers as they are placed onto the screen, with overlapping objects appearing more or less where they are placed by the designer. Earlier browsers, however, cannot interpret layers and absolute positioning, so Dreamweaver can reconvert layers to tables for backwards compatibility. To ensure that pages appear as closely as possible to the original layout, however, layers should not overlap as these cannot be converted into clean tables.

Before creating our home page, it is much easier to set up frames within Dreamweaver without having to hand-code a frameset. To do this, go to Modify, Frameset, Split Frame Up. This will produce a frame in the middle of the page that can be shifted to row 80 simply by dragging it up the page or changing the Row value to 80 in the Properties palette. From here, change the setting of Borders to Yes and set the value of the border to 0 to make the frame seamless. Simply clicking No may result in a white line between the two frames.

Next, save the pages and frameset. First of all, go to File, Save Frameset and give it the name default.html in the root folder. After this, click in each of the two frames and save the top one as header.html and the bottom one as home.html. We must now provide these two frames with names so that our links can be set to target the bottom frame. Alt-click (Windows) or option-click (Mac) each frame in turn, and in the Properties palette give them the names head and body and set the head frame to resize and no scrolling. Finally, set the background colours and link colour for each frame to the shades of green #009900 and #99FF99, by going to Modify, Page Properties and clicking on the Background colour tab, and give the page the title Kernow web site.

To add rollover buttons to the top frame, make sure that the cursor is in the header and click on the Insert Table button in the Object palette. Set the properties to 1 row, 6 columns with no cell spacing, padding or border, and the width to 600 pixels. With the table selected, change its alignment to centre, and then add the same images and links as defined in 'Adding frames to our site' above. The target for each link, located beneath the link button in the Properties palette, should be set to body so that each page loads in the bottom part of the screen.

Now that our header is set up, we need to add our image cross.gif and links to the bottom half of the page. Use the Insert Image button to place the cross on the page, then click on the cross and select the middle alignment from the Properties palette. Beneath this, enter the text History, Places, Where to Stay, Secret Cornwall and Search, hitting tab between each one before highlighting them and assigning relevant links.

Using templates, styles and libraries

When creating pages for a web site with Dreamweaver, there are several tools designed to enhance productivity, including templates, style sheets and libraries.

To use templates, create a new page and insert a layer 600 pixels wide to hold a grid for the history page. This will contain the same images and text as used for the page history.html when created in Composer. When images and text have been formatted, links entered for top-level pages and background images and link colours set, the entire page may be saved as a template by selecting File, Save as Template and then giving the page an appropriate title, such as basic page. Going to the site manager will reveal a new folder called Templates in which this file is stored.

When a template is created, the default setting is that sections cannot be edited so that consistency is ensured across a site. While our links to top-level pages will not be changed, the images and text entered into the main grid need to be updated for each page: to make this section editable, select the table holding these components and go to Modify, Templates, Mark Selection as Editable. Such sections will now appear in blue. To create a new page, go to File, New From Template and select this template: non-editable regions are now indicated in light yellow, but other sections of the page may be selected and modified.

In addition to using templates to speed up production work, Dreamweaver uses a Library to store commonly used elements. Clicking on the Library button on the Launcher palette will display a library and template window. If you create a new page, the template can be dragged from this window onto a page. The library stores individual components and, to add these to the library, select the image, table, text or link you wish to include and click on Create in the Library window; provide a name for each item and you will then be able to drag and drop standard items onto each new page.

Dreamweaver also includes tools that integrate the process of creating an image map. If you create a new page called places.html and insert the graphic map.jpg, you can add an image map to this picture by clicking on the Map button in the Properties palette. This displays a dialog box from where you can draw directly onto the image, indicating links to new pages. Once these are entered, provide a name for your image map and click OK.

5
Production:
dynamic content

In the vast majority of cases, people do not visit sites to marvel at the latest technology, but to find information, buy products or services and be entertained. What this means is that content is the most important feature of a web site. As Stephen Davies, Director of Strategy for Novell Europe and the commissioner of the yearly Novell Web 100 report, points out, 'if you can't get the information you require, you're not going to return to a site'.

This does not mean that a site's appearance is unimportant, but that good design is centred on making content usable, by making it clear where a visitor should go to find what they need. What is more, one of the main virtues of the web is interactivity. This is usually interpreted to mean feedback in the form of rollover buttons and animations; while important, interactivity can be implemented on web sites in a much more profound way, to process the information held on a site in response to visitors' enquiries. This chapter will therefore explore some of the ways in which content can be made truly dynamic on a site, using the Common Gateway Interface (CGI) and scripting.

Not that dynamic content relies purely on technology. The most successful sites of this exciting new medium are those which offer some value-added service, whether simplifying access to other sites as with portals such as Excite and Yahoo!, offering searchable databases of news like the *Guardian*'s Newsunlimited.com or the *Electronic Telegraph*, or simply providing a novel form of entertainment such as the bizarre but popular Hamster Dance (www.hamsterdance.com).

DYNAMIC WEB SITES

The web site outlined so far in this book is a relatively static entity: pages can be updated, of course, but the HTML files uploaded to a server will not change unless replaced. While this is more than sufficient to produce a great deal of useful content, dynamic web sites, which use server-based applications to respond to requests from the client browser and then generate a page dynamically, have much greater potential. Such dynamic page generation can be as simple as including a page counter that changes each time the page is accessed, or as complex as processing forms, personalising pages and returning results based on output from a search engine or database.

Using CGI

Building such interactive and dynamic web sites generally requires the use of Common Gateway Interface scripts and programs. We have already looked at some of the processes involved in scripting using JavaScript, which is a client-side means of making web pages more dynamic: that is, the script is downloaded with the web page and interpreted by the browser. CGI, on the other hand, runs an application on the server before returning its results to the browser, meaning that pages can change in response to information from the user.

Typical uses for server-side scripting include the following:

- **Forms:** Probably the most common use for server-side scripting is form processing whereby scripts take information from an HTML form, reading (or *parsing*) the data to post it to another user or an application on the server. Such scripts also usually provide a feed-back page to the user.

- **Personalised content:** An increasing number of web sites are setting up personalised pages that can store the preferences indicated by visitors to those sites. For example, news sites will often provide links to sports pages for certain visitors, or political news for others. Such preferences are recorded either in **cookies** (text files) stored on the visitor's computer, or in a registration database.

- **Search engines and databases:** One area where the web is extremely useful is for connecting web pages to databases, such as product catalogues or contact listings. At its simplest, a web site will include a search engine to scan pages on the site, but more complex databases will also allow users to organise and rearrange information, for example to list entries by date or location.

- **Security:** Security on a web site is, without scripting, a question of setting permissions on directories and files so that a visitor without appropriate permissions will receive an 'unauthorised access' message. With scripting, however, visitors can sign up online and set or receive a password, which they can then also change at other times.

- **E-commerce:** One of the most important uses for server-side scripting is e-commerce. More or less impossible without server-side scripting, e-commerce employs database controls to access stock catalogues and also to process orders.

How CGI works

When a browser requests a page from a server, it does not know a great deal about the documents it asks for, simply submitting a URL and interpreting the information that is returned. The server supplies certain codes using the Multipurpose Internet Mail Extensions (**MIME**) specifications, which enable the browser to interpret different types of information – such as a graphic which is displayed or a zip file that is saved to disk. The server generally only sends documents and tells the browser what type of file is being transmitted, but it can also launch other applications. When a browser submits a URL that points to a file, the server sends back that file; when the URL points to a program the server launches that application.

Using the Common Gateway Interface (CGI) specification, the server can read and write data to disk, storing variables that may produce different results each time the application runs (for example with a page counter). Typically, documents on a server are read-only for the majority of users, with owners having the ability to write over the file – after all, there is very little point in developing a site if any visitor is able to delete the contents of your site.

As well as read and write permissions, however, files may have a third property: whether they are executable. To be useful, CGI files (often referred to as scripts) must be executed, that is they must launch, process data and, typically, write out the results of that process. Depending on the type of server, CGI files may be located in one directory, usually known as the cgi-bin folder, from the day when all applications were referred to as binaries, or may be executed anywhere on the system.

Typically, scripts are placed in one directory, as this tends to be more secure than allowing programs to be launched from any directory on the system. Before such data is processed, however, it needs to be gathered, which will require some sort of form on your web site.

USING FORMS

Netscape introduced HTML forms as a means of data collection across the web, with information being processed on servers using CGI scripts. The form contains various controls, such as input fields and push buttons so that, when the 'submit' button is clicked, a data string is sent back to the server. For this information to be processed requires access to CGI routines, but it is also possible to use simple mail routines to pass information on or to use JavaScript to send information between pages or guide a visitor to different parts of the site.

Creating forms

A form is an area of a web page defined by the <FORM> ... </FORM> tag, which contains the various input controls and fields added to that page, as well as other images and text. The most important optional attributes to the <FORM> tag are ACTION and METHOD, which, as we have already seen, control communication between the form and the server using CGI.

Within these form tags can be placed six data-control types: single-line text fields, multiple-line text areas, drop-down selection lists, push buttons, check boxes and radio buttons. For all types other than multiple-line text areas and drop-down lists (which have their own tags), each control is defined by the <INPUT> tag with the attribute TYPE=, followed by 'text', 'button', 'checkbox' and 'radio'. There are also 'submit' and 'reset' attributes for buttons to send information or clear a form, as well as an input type called 'hidden', which does not appear on a screen but inserts a string in any information sent back to the server – invaluable if it has to handle more than one form. Multiple-line text areas use the <TEXTAREA> ... </TEXTAREA> tag, while drop-down lists are indicated by <SELECT> ... </SELECT>.

When creating a form control, each one must have another attribute, NAME, a description which is passed back to the server or in an email. Some will have other attributes, including VALUE, a default entry in a field or selected button, and SIZE and MAXLENGTH (the maximum number of characters in a field). <TEXTAREA> tags must also specify COL (columns), ROWS and WRAP (to control word-wrapping). <SELECT> tags must have an <OPTION> tag for each item that is to be entered into a drop-down list.

A simple form, therefore, could be constructed as follows:

```
<FORM ACTION="mailto:MyAddress"METHOD="POST">
Enter your name:
<INPUT TYPE="text", NAME="FullName"><P>
Where do you live? <BR>
<INPUT TYPE="radio" NAME="Continent"
VALUE="Europe" CHECKED>Europe<BR>
<INPUT TYPE="radio" NAME="Continent"
VALUE="America"> America<BR>
What computer do you use? <P>
<SELECT NAME="Computer">
<OPTION VALUE="PC">PC</OPTION>
<OPTION VALUE="Mac">Mac</OPTION></SELECT><P>
<INPUT TYPE="reset" NAME="reset" VALUE="Cancel">
<INPUT TYPE="submit" NAME="submit" VALUE="OK">
</FORM>
```

In the above example, the ACTION tag is slightly unusual: rather than pointing to a CGI script on the server, it uses the 'mailto:' attribute to post this form to a specified email address. This would be received as a text string looking something like the following (depending on information filled in by the visitor):

?FullName=John+Doe&Continent=Europe&Computer=PC&submit=OK

Processing forms

To be usable, the information in the above email must be 'parsed', elements stripped out for processing by a form or email. If the server the form is hosted on supports Perl, it is possible to use the script formail.pl, available from www.worldwidemart.com/scripts/. This script should be hosted in the cgi-bin folder and is extremely simple to customise: in a section near the beginning of the script, the user is asked to define variables; these include where the sendmail program (the UNIX application

that posts email) is – usually /usr/bin/sendmail or usr/sbin/sendmail –
and the domain name of the server.

To use formail.pl, the form itself requires some modification, particularly
the addition of a field called recipient with an email address for for-
mail.pl to forward the form results to, and either GET or POST as the
method to connect to the form, the address of which must be indicated
in the ACTION field. Thus the first two lines of our form above would
look like:

```
<FORM ACTION="http://www.myserver.com/cgi-bin/for-
mail.pl" METHOD="POST">
<INPUT TYPE="hidden" NAME="recipient"
VALUE="myname@myaddress.com">
```

When the Submit button is hit, formail creates a web page showing the
information entered by the user, which would be forwarded as an email
like the following:

```
Date: Sat, 23 Oct 1999 16:45:08 GMT
To: myname@myaddress
Subject: WWW Form Submission
Below is the result of your feedback form. It was
submitted by
() on Saturday, October 23, 1999 at 16:45:08
_____

FullName: John Doe
Continent: Europe
Computer: PC
Submit: OK
```

Form design

Visitors' experiences of using a form are affected by various design issues,
and it is easy to use forms inappropriately. For example, if users have to
fill in several forms across several pages before information is collected
and posted to the site manager only to be told on the last page that the
information can only be processed in a different browser (and there is at
least one e-commerce site I've encountered that does this), they are
unlikely to repeat the experience.

In addition to considering design across a site, forms will be affected by
page design, generally falling into the good, the bad and the ugly. Good

forms, as in Figure 5.1, should flow logically between different sections, so that as a visitor tabs from field to field he or she will not be confused by a cursor passing backwards and forwards on the page.

A poor form, as in Figure 5.2, will break up the logical sequence of fields, and be difficult to read. An ugly form is better in that it is usable, but lacks character: to improve such a form is really a question of using tables and colour or graphics to spruce up the page – but only after proper data-handling is established.

Adding a form to our site

Composer does not include tools for handling forms, so to create a form for our site the following example will use FrontPage Express. The first part of our page will consist of a list of three places of accommodation: open FrontPage Express and add the title Where_title.gif to the centre of the page after saving the page as where.html. Hit return and add a table consisting of three rows and two columns by clicking on the Insert Table button and dragging across two and down three. With the cursor in the table, go to Table, Table Properties and set the horizontal alignment of the table to the centre and the width to 600 pixels. Add the following images and text files:

- Cell 1: hotel.jpg/accomd1.txt
- Cell 2: self_cater.jpg/accomd2.txt
- Cell 3: bandb.jpg/accomd3.txt

We will now lay out a form with further details arranged in a table, which will be processed using formail.pl. To create the form, click on the one-line text box in the Forms toolbar (if you cannot see this toolbar, make sure it is selected under the View menu). Select and delete the text box that appears to leave the form area in place and, with the cursor in this area, create another table four rows deep but otherwise the same dimensions as the first table.

Place the cursor in the first cell and, from Table, Cell Properties, set the number of columns spanned to two. Delete the cell on the right-hand side and, in the remaining top cell, enter the text For further information please complete the following form:.

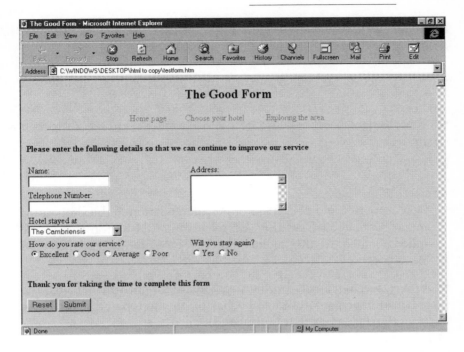

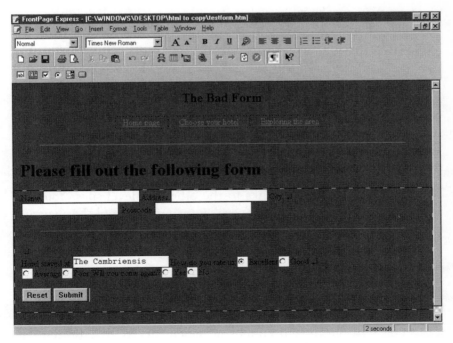

Figures 5.1 and 5.2   Examples of well- and poorly designed forms

In the four remaining cells, ensure that the vertical alignment of each is set to top and enter the following text and fields as in Figure 5.3:

- Row 2, left-hand cell: Name and Email, each with a one-line text box.

- Row 2, right-hand cell: Address and scrolling text box set to four lines deep.

- Row 3, left-hand cell: Season with four radio buttons labelled Spring, Summer, Autumn, Winter.

- Row 3, right-hand cell: Type of Accommodation and a drop-down menu. Double-click on this and select the Add button to add the following text to this menu: Hotels, Self-Catering and Bed and Breakfast.

- Row 4, left-hand cell: Two buttons, one to submit (the default), the other to reset the form (double click on the button and select Reset from the dialog box that is displayed).

Our form may now be processed in several ways. Right-click in the form and select Form Properties; in the dialog box that is displayed, the form can be given a name but, more importantly, an action provided to process information. In the box Form Handler, click on the Settings button; in the box for Action, enter either `mailto:myaddress` or type in the URL of the formail.pl script if you have access to a CGI folder. If you are using formail, in the box Hidden Fields you must click on the Add button and enter 'recipient' for name and an email address next to Value: this hidden field will be submitted with the form and provides the variable for formail.pl to post on the information it parses.

To complete the page, add links to the other top-level sites. You may also wish to experiment with the page's format, for example by changing text headings to green to match the colours across the rest of the site.

DYNAMIC COMPONENTS AND STYLES

Cascading style sheets

Cascading style sheets and current developments in XSL (eXtensible Style Sheets) are intended to distinguish between content creation and

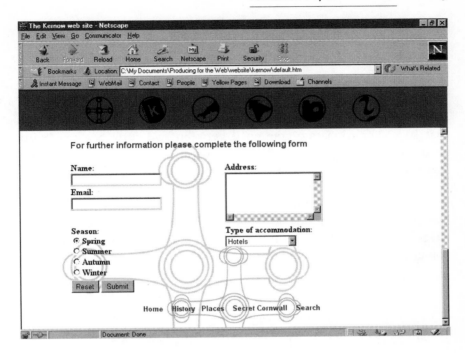

Figure 5.3   **The Kernow web form**

design in web production, with properties for such things as body text and links being established by style sheets; because these can be linked to external files across a web site, it is possible to create a single file that, when modified, will adjust all pages linked to it.

Style sheets are used only by version 4 browsers and above, and Internet Explorer and Netscape Navigator implement them slightly differently. However, elements of a CSS file that cannot be parsed by a browser are simply ignored, so that font, size and colour revert to the browser defaults. There are two types of style sheet: type 1 which controls the appearance of fonts and type 2 governing the positioning of text.

A style sheet is a text file with the ending .css that can be created in an ASCII text editor; the next step for our site is to create a simple CSS file that will determine the format of links on pages. Open Notepad or SimpleText and type in the following:

```
A{font-family:arial, helvetica, sans-serif;
font-size:10pt;
```

```
color:black;}
A:hover{color:white;}
```

Save the file as style1.css in the root directory, with default.html, header.html and home.html. The above file sets the font style, size and colour for any text contained between the tags <A> and </A>. Note that style definitions are contained between two curly brackets, with each property being separated from its definition by a colon and each line ending with a semicolon. The line A:hover changes the colour for a hyperlink when the cursor moves over text, an effect similar to using rollover images. This (at present) only works in Internet Explorer, Navigator simply ignoring this part of the style sheet. For the other pages on the site, save the file as style2.css and change the first font colour to green, the second (A:hover) to red.

The next step consists of providing a link to this style sheet within a web page. Open the file home.html in a text editor and enter the following line somewhere in the <HEAD> ... </HEAD> section:

```
<LINK REL="Stylesheet" HREF="style1.css"
TYPE="text/css">
```

For the other pages on the site, make the link to style2.css.

Search engines

One of the most useful features to add to a web site is a search engine, which, as its name implies, enables visitors to search for items by entering a query. There are two main types of search engine encountered on web sites: the first allows users to search the entire web and consists of a link to a major search engine such as Excite or AltaVista; the second, which is generally more useful, is a CGI linked to a script or a program running on the server which looks for matches to a query on the specific site.

There are various ways of including a search engine on your own site, and this section will cover one using a Perl script. The section 'Customising web-ready features' includes an alternative approach using FreeFind. As with many Perl CGI scripts, rather than creating a search engine from scratch it is possible to customise scripts that are available on the Internet. The following script demonstrates how to customise a very simple search engine called jasearch, by Jason Anthony and available on www.ufbs.co.uk. Another one using a similar approach is Simple Search, on www.worldwidemart.com/scripts.

Jasearch has two key components, the HTML search form and the script jasearch.pl. One of the virtues of this search engine is that the Perl script may require no modification at all, all variables being set within the HTML document. However, the file jasearch.pl must be uploaded to a working CGI directory and made executable (see 'Publishing and managing a site' in chapter six). In addition, the first line must point to where Perl is located, for example #!/usr/bin/perl. If Perl is not located at this point, you will need to contact the ISP to find the appropriate directory and change the script accordingly.

Most customisation, however, takes place in the HTML form, with full instructions at www.ufbs.co.uk. First of all, a form must be inserted on the page that includes the following code:

```
<FORM METHOD="POST" ACTION="/cgi-bin/jasearch.pl">
<INPUT TYPE="hidden" NAME="base" VALUE="../mydi-
rectory">
<INPUT TYPE="hidden" NAME="rbase"
VALUE="http://myaddress">
Search for <INPUT TYPE="TEXT" NAME="sv" VALUE="">
<INPUT TYPE="SUBMIT" VALUE="Search">
<INPUT TYPE="RESET" VALUE="Reset">
</FORM>
```

The first line indicates that data collected from the form is posted to the script jasearch.pl at the address /cgi-bin/jasearch.pl. Of the two variables that must be changed the first, 'base', refers to the directory on the server where the documents to be searched are contained. The next variable, 'rbase', is similar to the first but indicates the public URL that is searched. Beneath rbase is an input box where visitors enter their query – this must have the attribute NAME="sv" to work with jasearch.pl.

Once you have created a form with the above code, entering any relevant changes to background, images and textual information, the search form can be uploaded to your web site and a link made from the rest of the site to the search engine.

Adding a search form to our web site

Designing a page for our search engine is relatively simple, in that all it requires is a text box, Submit button and some instructions for use. The most difficult part using Composer is the fact that such a page requires a basic form, which can be hand-coded or, as with the form above, created using another editor such as FrontPage Express. We'll use the latter for the search page, as well as providing code for creating the same page in Composer.

First of all, open the file template.html and replace the title with search_title.gif and the default table with one that consists of one column 600 pixels wide and is one row deep in the centre of the page. If your ISP supports FrontPage extensions, completing the search form is as simple as clicking Insert, WebBot component and selecting Search. This displays a dialog box from which variables such as labels and box width are set, as well as whether the results page indicates a score or file size and date. When you click OK, the page will be completed; when the file is transferred to the server, it must be placed in a directory that can execute scripts.

If your ISP does not support FrontPage extensions, use jasearch.pl. Place the script in the appropriate cgi-bin folder as described above and insert a text box in the table (which also inserts a form). Add the text 'Search for' before this and insert a Submit and Reset button. Double-click on the text box and enter "sv" for the Name then click on View, HTML, and enter the relevant information outlined above in the <FORM> tab. Your form should look like Figure 5.4.

The code for this search form, then, is as follows:

```
<TABLE BORDER="0" WIDTH="600">
  <TR>
  <TD><FORM ACTION="http://myaddress/cgi-
bin/jasearch.pl" METHOD="POST">
<INPUT TYPE="HIDDEN" NAME="BASE" VALUE="..kernow/
pages/">
<INPUT TYPE="HIDDEN" NAME="RBASE"
VALUE="http://myaddress/kernow/pages/">
<INPUT TYPE="HIDDEN" NAME="BACKGROUND"
VALUE="../kernow/images/backgrnd.gif">
<p>Search for <INPUT TYPE="text" SIZE="20"
NAME="sv"> </p>
```

```
<p><INPUT TYPE="submit" VALUE="Search">
<INPUT TYPE="reset" VALUE="Reset"> </p>
</FORM></TD>
</TR>
</TABLE>
```

Dynamic HTML

To complete our site, we will add the final Secret Cornwall page which makes use of certain dynamic HTML effects to create an interactive site. Composer, being a 3.2 compliant HTML editor, is not able to construct DHTML pages. This example uses Dreamweaver, which offers a huge amount of support for DHTML effects, but other good editors include GoLive, HoTMetaL Pro, FrontPage 2000 (not Express) and Fusion. Our dynamic page makes use of layers to hide and display information when a cursor is moved over a map: because these layers are not converted to tables, such pages will not display in version 3 browsers.

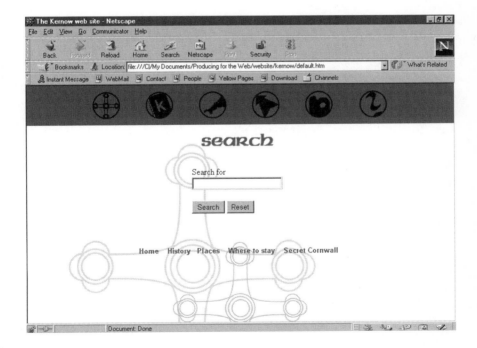

Figure 5.4   **The Kernow search page**

Dynamic effects, like JavaScript, are attached to events that can be triggered by mouse movements. As the events in this example are produced by the cursor moving over parts of an image, the image must first be sliced so that different sections can cause different effects. If you have a program such as ImageReady or Fireworks to hand, download the image penwith.jpg and open it in one of these applications: using mask tools, each program can create guidelines for slicing the image as well as generating the HTML code to incorporate the image within a web page. There are full instructions on how to image-slice using these programs on the web site under the techniques section. Alternatively, download the different penwith_r_*.jpg files and the file penwith_table.htm and cut and paste it into a template file named map.html.

The sliced image should be positioned in the centre of the page, with the file penwith_title.gif and links to each of the top-level pages beneath it. The images in the table contain four yellow circles and four red stars corresponding to different places that display hidden text on the page. Using the Insert Layer tool, draw four boxes on each side of the map, copying the files penwith1-8.txt into each box. Once text is entered, select each layer and, in the Properties box, set the visible setting to 'hidden'. It is generally easier to work with multiple layers if they are given distinctive names, and you can change the name for each layer in the Properties palette.

After making each layer invisible, select the star or circle that corresponds to each one and select the behaviours in the Layers and Behaviors window. At the top of this window are plus and minus buttons to add and remove dynamic effects (or behaviours) to web pages. Click on the plus button and select Show-Hide Layers: a dialog box appears with the names of each layer and buttons to hide or show each layer. Select Show for each layer.

The default event to trigger dynamic effects is onMouseDown (that is, clicking the mouse), but pressing the small arrow next to onMouseDown will reveal a number of other events, including onMouseOver, which is the one needed to trigger a layer becoming visible. Objects may have more than one event associated with them: click the Plus button again and this time select Hide for each layer, caused this time by the onMouseOut event. You could continue to add further events: for example, by carefully changing the colour of each circle or star, it would be possible to create rollover buttons that would light up as the mouse moved over them, as well as display hidden layers.

Save the page and preview it in a 4.0 compatible browser or later; it should look like Figure 5.5. As the mouse moves over the different icons in the central map, so different layers should become visible and disappear on the page, displaying text relevant to each part of the map. DHTML can be used to animate layers, moving them around the screen in response to mouse movements or clicks, as well as making different layers visible or invisible. The fact that Communicator and Internet Explorer implement such things as layers and other DHTML effects in slightly different ways, however, means that such effects are generally under-utilised on the web because it is very easy to generate errors if a visitor is using a different server. The moral is: if you wish to use DHTML, be prepared to spend a great deal of time debugging pages.

CUSTOMISING WEB-READY FEATURES

The CGI features discussed in this chapter require access to a cgi-bin folder or FrontPage extension support. In many cases, however, CGI support is not available in this way (the web site is being hosted on

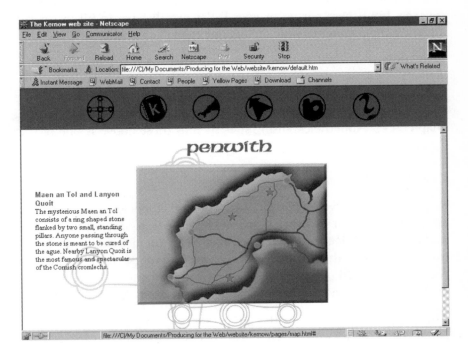

Figure 5.5 **Displaying hidden layers with DHTML**

student space or a free web-space server, for example). Nonetheless, third-party support often exists to make web sites more dynamic.

Links to servers hosting these features can be placed in a web page so that the visitor's browser follows the link. Thus a guestbook page may look like part of your site, but is actually being hosted on a completely different server. Many of these services are effectively free to the producer, being paid for by supporting advertisements.

Web counters

Web counters offer a means of keeping track of the number of visitors to your site. The <IMG> tag on the page links to a virtual image file which is calculated by the web counter server: visitors to the page request the image from the server, which is intercepted by the counter server and a graphic generated according to the number of hits stored in its file.

Many ISPs provide hit counters as part of their hosting service, and it is always worth using these as first choice. LinkExchange offers a counter service with statistics at www.bcentral.com/fastcounter, while www.the-counter.com offers a fast service with no advertisements. Whether using counters from these parties or your ISP, you will have to fill in a form directing the counter to your site or copy the HTML code.

Web counters are not as neat a feature as they appeared about six years ago: if not enough people visit your site a web counter announcing the fact can appear foolish, and the important task of assessing how many visitors is better done by examining log files (see 'Auditing site use' in chapter six). Nonetheless, using sites such as those above is one of the easiest ways of learning some of the principles of CGI.

Guestbooks

A guestbook is a section of the web where visitors can leave messages and view those left by other visitors. The HTML to display these messages has to be calculated by the server each time a message is added and then returned to the browser. As with web counters, the link on your page is to a virtual page on the server which is intercepted by the guestbook server and the appropriate data page generated.

There are various third-party guestbook servers, such as www.the-guestbook.com, www.websiteresources.net/guestbook and www.-glacier-web.com. Some of these can be customised with personal graphics and captions, and display banner advertisements.

Like web counters, guestbooks tend to be rather superficial in terms of feedback, although there are times when a guestbook can serve a useful function as a focus for people sharing an interest. In general, however, forums are more useful.

Search forms

We have already looked at the possibility of creating a search form on our site using a Perl script. It is also possible to use third-party search engines that send out a 'spider' to explore your site before compiling an index: when a visitor enters a query, it is passed to that site which checks its index and returns the results. Again, third-party search engines such as www.freefind.com and www.beseen.com finance themselves through the use of banners.

Offering the ability to search your site is probably one of the most advantageous interactive services you can add, which is why we spent so much time on it earlier in this chapter.

Response forms

Retrieving information from users can be essential for an interactive service on a site, such as collecting details for sending out purchases or information. While HTML forms are easy to create, however, (see 'Creating forms' above), to provide feedback to visitors and post on the information to the site producer requires server-side scripts. Typically, such scripts send the form to a specified email address, once the visitor has filled in all relevant details, and then sends a 'thank you' page to the visitor.

Once again, there are several third-party services which can process information for you, including www.freedback.com, www.responders.net and www.response-o-matic.com. Note: again these free services use advertisements to finance them, which in the case of freedback are quite garish.

Forms, again, are generally helpful when used well. In addition to using third-party feedback services, you can of course use JavaScript to navigate between pages if you do not have access to a cgi-bin directory.

Forums and chat

Forums (or bulletin boards/newsgroups) provide the ability for visitors to a site to post a message to which other visitors can reply, building up discussion threads. Building up forums via CGI scripts is complex, but once again there is third-party support for forums, such as www.beseen.com and network54.com. As with guestbooks, forum databases are stored on the third-party server: the link from a page is intercepted by this server which sends HTML back to the visitor's browser.

Internet Relay Chat allows people to exchange live messages that appear as messages in a scrolling window to which visitors can add their own comments. There are servers such as www.parachat.com that will host a chat channel for free with banners. When such pages are opened, the client is downloaded (usually as a Java applet usable with the browser) and connects to that site's channel on the server.

Although they tend to be complicated to set up, chat and forum areas on a site can encourage considerable feedback and tend to be popular with a wide range of visitors. If you are responsible for a web site, however, it is worth bearing in mind that it is easy for a forum or chat site to quickly leave your control if it is not moderated – that is part of the fun, but may be more difficult if you are running a web site for an organisation.

CONTENT CREATION

So far, we have concentrated on the technical aspects of site design, but technical skills do not make a successful site on their own. Indeed, in the vast majority of cases, visitors to a site will not fire up their browsers and type in your URL to gape open-mouthed at how you implement the latest technologies; as with consumers of other media, whether it be print, television or cinema, their first concern is content.

Various pundits have suggested that the successful web sites of the future will be those which offer useful services, such as selling goods more conveniently than over the phone or in person, or which are content rich. This is why media providers such as the BBC (www.bbc.co.uk), the *New York Times* (www.nyt.com) or Pathfinder (www.pathfinder.com) are placing so much of their content online. The idea is that, at present, users may be unwilling to pay for content, but when a fifty-year-old database becomes a fully searchable archive the text and graphics we tend to treat as ephemeral are suddenly given a new lease of life.

CONTENT UNBOUND: BRITANNICA ONLINE

One of the most remarkable indications of the future of online production comes from one of the oldest and most respected content providers in the Western world – the *Encyclopaedia Britannica* (www.britannica.com). Founded in Edinburgh in 1768, over the following two centuries *Britannica* was one of *the* books that defined publishing. During the 1990s, with the spread of CD-ROM, print encyclopaedias came to be seen as increasingly costly and lacked the search facilities of the new medium.

Britannica was then published online and on CD – but at considerable cost (approximately £700 in 1995) to preserve sales of the printed version. Within a couple of years, and losing out to upstarts such as *Encarta*, the cost of *Britannica* plummeted, but even this did not prepare for the sudden release of the free online version, funded through advertising and deals with Barnes and Noble for book sales. At the time of writing, competitors such as *Encarta* have begun to follow suit, and concerns have been raised about the possibility that the quality of the information provided will suffer. Nonetheless, as part of the gift economy of the Internet, this is one of the most remarkable resources that has shifted from paper to the screen.

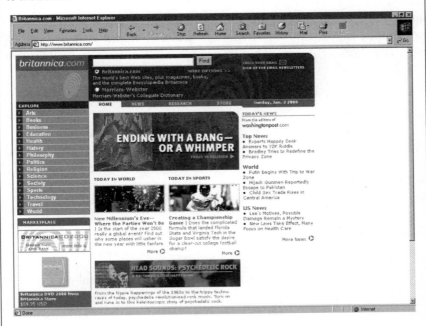

Figure 5.6   Britannica Online – the encyclopaedia of the future?

Setting the style

As well as becoming a content-provider, successful web development depends on developing an appropriate style for the presentation of material. Such a style depends on establishing an audience and cultivating a distinctive voice, and the basics of developing a good style cannot be repeated often enough: revise and edit your work and master the basics of punctuation and grammar. Demonstrating skills in DHTML and Flash may count for nothing if public perception of your pages is based on an inability to spell.

In many cases, the best style is often that which is clearest and plainest (though these are not synonymous). There is no reason why you should stick to such a style – after all, many world-famous writers are florid, metaphorical and elaborate – but if your desire is to appeal to as wide an audience as possible, you should write appropriately. As Matthew Arnold commented, 'Have something to say, and say it as clearly as you can. That is the only secret of style.'

Expanding on Arnold's advice, in most cases it is advisable to write as you speak but more precisely, paying attention to rules of grammar and avoiding colloquialisms unless they are relevant. Note, however, that simplicity in good writing is often more apparent than real, concealing painstaking art behind its artlessness. Indeed, clarity is often not the same as plainness; it can elaborate a subject but does so by avoiding jargon as much as possible.

In conclusion, then, the style must be appropriate to the subject: it should not rise above content, but be the means of expressing content in as lively, clear and vivid a manner as possible. Sometimes a provocative and opinionated writing style may be the best way to attract readers. If you are writing copy for an online catalogue, however, you should be as self-effacing as possible, offering information as clearly and as succinctly as possible to visitors.

Selecting an audience

Which leads on to the question of establishing an audience. For example, when publishing news (which has been very successful on the web) there must be facts to report but, equally important, these must appeal to readers. One useful tip is to look at what is currently being published to see what is on offer. Remember that a story is something that is crafted and also has an angle.

How do you determine a market on the web? The first step should be to look at what is available across the Internet. There are many sites that offer some sort of editorial. Some of these, such as *Time* (www.-time.com), simply offer the same material that is available in another medium. Others, such as *Hotwired* (www.hotwired.lycos.com) or *Slate* (www.slate.com), develop original material that is aimed at a specific audience looking for material on the Internet. Do not neglect other media that offer a style or appeal to an audience you wish to address.

Many home pages or amateur sites offer factual information, or a provocative stance on certain issues, or locate other people who share similar enthusiasms. One of the virtues of the web is that 'professionals' have not always staked out the relevant territory in advance; for example, in my own field of computer journalism, one site that has gained a great deal of respect is Tom's Hardware page (www.tomshardware.com), which carries a large number of computer news items and reviews and has even developed into a semi-professional venture generating revenue through advertising.

Crafting stories

News stories have been one particularly successful form of content on the web. There are several reasons for this, such as the ability to update information on a regular basis and to search through stories, but also the fact that news writing tends to pack a considerable amount of information into a relatively short space. While sites such as the Gutenberg Project (www.promot.net/pg/) perform an admirable task of transferring classic texts online, few people want to read *War and Peace* on their screens.

Such journalistic writing also offers some useful tips for developing a style appropriate for the web: introductions to stories should be short and punchy, containing relevant information in the first twenty or thirty words. This 'news pyramid' traditionally enabled editors to cut stories from the bottom up so that important information would not be omitted. On the web, this is made doubly important because readers may click on a link to a different page before completing the story.

When developing such a pyramid, it is common to provide a brief statement that summarises the story, followed by a more extensive repetition of the introduction (often called the pivot paragraph which explains what the story is about) before finally expanding the details of the story in the main body of text. This is not the only way to develop a story, especially as a good story should have a dramatic ending, but on a web site it may be useful to extend the story over several pages rather than have one long page (particularly if there are images) which readers have to download before they can assess its value. Bear in mind that it can be much more difficult for most people to read text on screen rather than on paper: as a general rule of thumb, text that spans more than two screens may be tiring to read.

As Nicholas Bagnall has remarked in his book *Newspaper Language* (1993): 'Everyone knows the old saying: if you can't get their attention in the first sentence (or the first eight seconds) they won't bother with the rest.' At the same time, a web site should offer the opportunity to explore, to allow the reader to determine their own pathways through which stories are interesting. A person who has bought a newspaper has, in some sense, already committed themselves to looking through it, however cursorily; the same is not true of a site on the Internet.

Storytelling techniques

Introductions to stories may consist of a narrative or anecdote, descriptive scene-setting, provocative statements, or a quote or question. Endings tend to restate or refer to the beginning. The classic example is the detective story where the gun on a table in the opening paragraph is used to shoot someone in the final scene. It is not always practical to have a story that is so tightly plotted, but a good conclusion to a piece will progress ideas in the text as well as restate them.

A common technique is to include single-line headings or descriptions with a link to the relevant story: if the reader is curious, they will follow that link. While it may seem unfair for your hours, days and weeks of work to be dismissed with a single click, an important technique for maximising a site is to create as many internal links as possible. Visitors will generally make their mind up about a page within a few seconds before hitting the back button or another link: if those links lead to attractive-sounding pages on your own site, you may be able to build up a wider readership than by insisting that visitors trudge through every page before deciding whether to stay.

Use boxes, bullet points, panels, sidebars and tables to offer information at a glance. Frequently readers will skim through an article looking at such things as pull-quotes (where a line of text is displayed in larger type), captions and boxes to see if the story is interesting before return-ing to the main body text. These various panels and boxes can sum-marise the information contained in an article or expand on additional information not dealt with in the main copy.

Prepare for an audience, but don't slavishly follow a formula – allow for surprises. There is no single formula that can cover every story, every article and review, every feature. Bear in mind that some of the most interesting articles will include information that the reader does not already know. Regarding writing style, the flow of content is important, especially if the text is fact-heavy, and one of the best ways of establish-ing whether copy flows is to re-read material on a regular basis, to stop being a writer and *become a reader*.

TIPS FOR CONTENT CREATION

- **Select an audience:** While not necessary in the sense that you may wish to cre-ate a web site entirely for your own benefit and to express your own interests, having a clear idea of the audience you wish your site to appeal to can be helpful in terms of producing appropriate text and other content.

- **Write as you speak:** Or, to be more accurate, write as you would speak but more precisely. In most cases, this is the best way to produce clear, readable copy. Avoid jargon and aim for clarity.

- **Use the pyramid:** A technique from news journalism: offer a summary of your story at the beginning and expand from there. While this was useful to subs who needed to cut stories from the end, it is useful on the web not to save space (which is almost never an issue) but for readers who may wish to move on to other pages.

- **Use links:** A good way to keep visitors on a site is to give them lots to visit. You can't guarantee to provide everything for everyone on one page, so include plenty of links to other parts of your site.

- **Become a reader:** Read and revise your copy on a regular basis.

Ethics of content production

Because of its nature as a novel, international medium, the Internet in general and the web in particular have raised questions about the ethics of their method of communication. Most of the debate has concentrated around the issues raised by copyright infringement, libel and obscenity.

Copyright

A common assumption is that the ability to download something makes it freely available. This is not the case, although many people who break the copyright law on the Internet do so inadvertently. For example, a photo or article may be posted to a newsgroup without the original author's consent – even if the person posting the material is not paid for transmission the act remains an offence. The British government, for example, has recently drafted legislation extending copyright and 'fair use' (similar to the rules covering photocopying) to digital distribution.

One form of digital distribution that has aroused a huge amount of controversy recently is MP3, where distributors have attempted to crack down on the illegal pirating of music. So widespread was the distribution of CD-quality MP3 files across the web that several search engines recorded the term as being a more popular entry than sex in 1999.

Responses to MP3 have generally consisted of attempting to introduce alternative formats that can be copyright-protected but, at the time of writing, these have not been particularly successful. Music piracy has long been an issue, with companies taking a percentage of the cost of a blank tape to cover anticipated illegal uses, but digital piracy is perceived as being a much worse potential threat because sound quality does not deteriorate with multiple copies.

With regard to MP3 piracy, most small acts are not pursued – that is, should you copy a soundtrack from a CD into MP3 format on your hard drive you are as likely to attract official attention as by making a tape for the car. However, distributing that file to an FTP site on the Internet is a different matter, and attempts to regulate piracy have concentrated less on individuals than on the sites hosting illicit material. What this means in practice is that illegal MP3 sites tend to disappear very quickly, partly as a result of their being swamped by visitors and also because it is easier to take an ISP to court. With regard to placing illegally copyrighted material on your own web sites, whether it is music, images or text, small cases may go unnoticed but it is not worth the risk of having a site closed down if you wish to use it for professional or commercial purposes.

Although it is not impossible to regulate copyright on the web, however, the sheer ease and nature of digital copying almost certainly means that laws designed for older media will have to be rethought if they are to succeed in this digital medium.

Libel

As well as copyright issues, beware of libel. Writers and critics are not immune to libel laws, and simply because you publish a web site without making profit does not mean that you may not be taken to court. There is, however, a defence against libel in the form of 'fair comment'. This allows someone to be as harsh in their criticism as they like so long as it is honest opinion. There is, however, the possibility of this defence turning into catch-22, with the writer being damned if they publish their honest opinion because the person or company libelled disagrees.

Until 1999, there had been little significant legislation concerning libellous statements on the Internet, though some figures had received out-of-court settlements for statements circulated on email or newsgroups. For example, Norwich Union agreed to pay the Western Provident Association (WPA) £450,000 for comments made in an internal email that, WPA argued, was defamatory. The case brought by Dr Laurence Godfrey against Demon and discussed in chapter one has also focused the attention of Internet publishers on the issue of libel.

When using the defence of fair comment, it is important to get the facts right: opinion is not the same as fact, so that saying an item is too expensive and then quoting the wrong price will not be helpful if you are later sued. Secondly, and this is often the most difficult part of defending against libel, an opinion that is judged excessive – such as calling someone obese who has put on a couple of pounds – may not be held to be honest opinion. Likewise, if there is a chance that your writing may be motivated by malice, such as a review of work by your ex-partner, it is probably advisable not to publish.

The last test of honest opinion is whether a piece of work is in the public interest. If you are writing about something that has been published or distributed such as a book, interview or film, then this is usually less of a problem than reciting gossip about a figure who may not be in the public domain.

Obscenity

For most web designers, copyright will be the largest problem when creating content. However, part of the excitement of the Internet revolves
around its status as the largest uncensored mass medium in history.
Scare stories of paedophilia, terrorism and racism abound on the
Internet or, more usually, in other media discussing the Internet. There
are unsavoury, and even criminal, sites on the web, but not necessarily
to the saturation point indicated by such stories.

Whilst the argument in America has polarised between those advocating free speech whatever the cost and those advocating censorship
whatever the cost, attempts to introduce such things as the
Communications Decency Act as part of wider telecommunications
bills have demonstrated some of the difficulties for the US government
(or any other national government) in policing the web effectively.

Not that regulation is impossible. As discussed in chapter one, the case
of *Regina* v. *Waddon*, brought before Southwark Crown Court, made
some steps towards considering what constitutes a publication on the
web. In that case, an act of publication was held to take place when the
defendant transmitted material to the ISP, meaning that placing
obscene material on a server in another country does not make the person immune from prosecution in this country. Probably the most important point for a web producer is that it begins to clarify what constitutes
a publication on the Internet.

6

Post-production

Once a site has been designed, it must be tested and transferred to a networked computer for others to access it, either an intranet server or one connected to the Internet. Testing is an important part of the process: dead links, loading errors, elements that do not display properly in different browsers – these and other problems if not identified will probably cause visitors to dismiss your site and not return.

Furthermore, it is extremely rare for a web site, once published, not to be updated and yet this is something that is not always considered at the planning stage. This chapter will therefore address issues relating to maintaining and developing a site as well as tools to publish it to the web. In particular, as UNIX remains the backbone of the web in terms of an operating system, yet is rarely encountered by desktop users familiar with Windows or MacOS, we will cover some of the intricacies of using UNIX's powerful command line interface.

Finally, once your web site is online, you need to attract visitors using search engines, newsgroups and even advertising. The temptation for a web producer is to assume that once a page is uploaded to a site your work is over: in most cases it will be just beginning.

TESTING AND MANAGING A WEB SITE

Usefulness and usability

> It's easy for a computer to offer operations that don't help people.
> Thomas Landauer, The Trouble with Computers (1995)

Landauer has written extensively about the failure of information technology to deliver on many of its promises, a problem that is not so much to do with the limitations of computers as with a failure by programmers to test their applications against the expectations of users. As Landauer remarks, it is all too easy for a programmer or computer designer, who almost by definition will *love* computers, to have little time for the end-user who may be forced to employ that program because of his or her job.

The process of testing, in a sense, takes us back to the pre-production issues discussed in chapter two. Having made a plan for our web site (ideally in consultation with a client or supervisor) and then built the site, the next step is to test the product before releasing it into the wild. I use the term advisedly: 'releasing into the wild' is an expression frequently used to describe the process by which viruses are distributed to roam at large – and there are some sites which probably count as an information virus in terms of spreading frustration and bad practice.

Testing your site, therefore, is a feedback process: if a page does not work, or users cannot see the point of a site or find information they need, individual pages may need to be redesigned or, in extreme cases, the entire site taken back to the drawing board. Consequently, it is advisable to test throughout the production process to ensure that development is not too far advanced if a major glitch emerges.

When testing, two key terms from Landauer are helpful: usefulness and usability. The two terms are not synonymous, although a useful site that offers information or services that users need is likely to be less useful if it is unusable, that is visitors cannot access information. On the other hand, it is easy to create a usable site that can be navigated easily yet offers nothing worthwhile to visitors.

The most important testing that can be done – but which is often neglected by web producers – is to use a variety of browsers and even machines if possible. See what your page looks like in different versions of IE and Communicator, and if there is any difference on a Mac and a PC. Bear in mind also that browser users can set certain effects such as text size and links to their own specifications. What effect will this have on the overall appearance of your site?

Finally, test at every stage of production – what is known as formative testing. Designers may be good at testing their product at the end – summative testing – but formative testing is important to the feedback process of ongoing development.

Links and updates

More general considerations about site testing for a producer revolve around the integrity of the site structure, whether such things as links will continue to work, both internally to other pages, images and files, and to external sites. This can take some time to establish, particularly with large sites, as the amorphous nature of the web means that links to pages must be checked on a regular basis.

If a site is substantial in terms of size, this is the point where investing in a web editor such as Dreamweaver, GoLive or FrontPage can pay dividends. These applications include management and reporting tools that can test each link, including ones to external sites if the test computer is online, and highlight dead links. Likewise, they include global search and replace tools, and the usefulness of templates in an application such as Dreamweaver really comes into its own at this point: changing an element of the template will also make changes to pages that use that template, streamlining the producer's work considerably.

As well as testing the structure of your site, ensure that you have a plan to regularly test and update the efficacy of your site's content. This will vary greatly from site to site. For example, a series of pages offering an outline of the life and work of Charles Dickens may not require updating very often if it is simply offered as the producer's opinion on that author: then again, if it is intended as a scholarly site, it may need to include updates on a monthly or quarterly basis to take into account new research. A news service, on the other hand, should have at least daily updates, and probably even hourly changes, or at least be updated as and when new stories break.

The important point is that you should have some sort of strategy where appropriate for developing your site to prevent it becoming redundant. This tends to be one of the areas that is most often overlooked, particularly for intranets and other services where a commercial benefit may not be immediately obvious yet labour and hours are required to keep the site up to date.

PUBLISHING AND MANAGING A SITE

Using FTP

Files are transferred across the web all the time using browsers and email applications, but these transfers are usually restricted to handling specific file types. To publish files to a server so that they can be viewed requires the use of File Transfer Protocol (FTP) software.

FTP, unlike email, is used to transfer files to a public server rather than between individuals. The big difference between the hypertext transfer protocol and FTP is that in the latter file transfer works both ways, uploading to as well as downloading from the server. FTP clients can be stand-alone programs such as WS_FTP for Windows or Fetch for Macs, or are incorporated into the browser with Navigator and Internet Explorer 5.

FTP requires little information about the type of file that is being sent, but it does have two modes for sending files: text and binary. The former is used to send ASCII text with no changes at all and is useful for transferring HTML files to a server. Binary can send any file type at all, which can cause problems with some text files: if an HTML file or Perl script, for example, is uploaded, it may not work correctly if the file originated on a Windows or MacOS system and is being transferred to a UNIX server, because the line endings are not preserved. In such cases, use text mode to transfer the files.

FTP applications

Browsers such as Internet Explorer 5 and Netscape Navigator include basic FTP capabilities that can be used to transfer files to and from a server as long as it is set up without any peculiarities (such as using a different port to the standard FTP port). To connect to an FTP server, enter the address in the browser which usually begins with ftp:// rather than http://; for a private directory on an ISP's server, this will usually be in the format ftp://userID:password@servername.

From the FTP server, downloading files simply consists of clicking on the selected file names. With Navigator, files can also be uploaded to a site from the menu option, File, Upload File. Using Internet Explorer 5, files can be transferred to a site by dragging and dropping them into the remote directory.

While these browsers allows users to perform basic FTP operations, the fact that they do not distinguish between binary and text files could be problematic, as is the fact that some FTP servers may use unconventional settings. In such circumstances, shareware FTP applications such as WS_FTP (www.ipswitch.com) provide a convenient graphical interface which works like Windows Explorer to drag and drop files between the local and remote hard drives.

Connection to a server is slightly different than with a web browser, providing more options as well as the address of the FTP server: this includes entering user names and passwords, as well as determining host types and the use of such features as a firewall. Once connection has been made, such applications display series of folders, whether the server is MacOS, Windows or UNIX based, enabling users to move files into appropriate directories.

Managing Windows NT sites

Once files are placed onto a site, directories and folders must be established to contain files, permissions set for files that need to be read or executed, and any old files deleted and cleared away. If the server you are using runs Windows NT (or a Mac server), managing the site will be familiar from using a desktop operating system such as Windows 95 or MacOS.

The complexities of using Windows NT are mainly the responsibility of the server administrator, and for producers placing files on that server the requirements for setting up accounts and other administrative functions are of little concern. When connecting to a remote server using FTP, however, there are certain features that every web producer should be aware of.

When you upload files onto a site using FTP, those files may be uploaded into an FTP directory and must then be moved into the appropriate area. Using an FTP application such as FTP Explorer, you can create new folders from within the program and then copy image files and pages to relevant directories.

Windows NT enables users to set permissions on different files down to the level of individual files as well as directories. This means that hidden files can co-exist in the same folder as publicly available web pages – for example, a section of a site that is only available to subscribers. In most cases, executable files, that is applications that must run on the server as well as be read by the browser, will be contained in a folder in which the permissions are set accordingly; it is highly unlikely, unless you have administrator privileges to the site, that you will be able to set a folder as executable. However, other files can be hidden by right-clicking on the file and changing the file properties.

Managing UNIX sites

While Windows NT is gaining ground as a web server, most servers on the Internet run the UNIX operating system to host sites. Although some ISPs only allow users to upload files to a directory on the server using FTP, some also provide access to the server to set up and maintain sites; indeed, some ISPs require files to be uploaded to a specific directory (to check for viruses, for example), and users then telnet into a machine to move files to another directory.

We will spend a little more time considering how to use UNIX than Windows because it is a very different environment from most PC and Mac operating systems and yet, because of its status as the main operating system for web servers, is one that you are likely to encounter. While UNIX and Linux can employ a graphical user interface (GUI), they are principally encountered across the Internet as command-line interfaces, that is instructions have to be typed in at a command prompt. This is what makes them very powerful, in that a whole range of processes can be set in motion simply by typing in a string of words and letters, which can be done much more quickly across a network than by manipulating images with a mouse.

Unfortunately, with the decline of DOS many users are unfamiliar with such commands and some system administrators use the rather derogatory term 'guicks' (pronounced 'gweeks') to refer to those who try to upload files to a UNIX server but have only ever encountered GUIs before. The following tips are therefore intended to help web producers get up to speed with UNIX as quickly as possible: you do not need to understand UNIX inside out to manage a web site, but you should know relevant commands and processes.

Using Telnet

Telnet is an Internet service that was extremely important in the days of bulletin boards, offering a text-based application to locate and download files: while most servers now use web pages for this type of information,

Telnet remains useful for logging into remote machines and managing sites, particularly as UNIX commands can be run from the text command line. Windows 95, 98 and NT include a Telnet application, while Mac users can download a copy of the NCSA Telnet application from archive sites such as TUCOWS (www.tucows.com).

To connect to a host computer, select Connect, Remote System and enter the name of the system to log on to (if you wish to try out Telnet, you can log on to the US Library of Congress at locis.loc.gov). The Port box should be left at Telnet in the vast majority of cases, and TermType again works in most cases with VT100 (the type of terminal that Telnet emulates). When connection is made, log on with the user name and password of your account, or guest if this is a public site.

When you have finished a session, it is advisable to type in exit at the command prompt rather than simply close the Telnet application.

UNIX commands

Once logged in to a server using Telnet, users see a prompt which is usually $, ~ (tilde) or % but may be another character. For those who have any experience using DOS, while some of the commands may be confusing the basic principle is the same: users navigate around the system and execute commands by typing in command words, some of which are the same as in DOS (such as cd to change directory), while others are slightly different (such as cp to copy a file). Another important difference between Windows and Mac machines is that UNIX uses the forward slash (/) to separate directories rather than the backward one (\ ).

Thus, for example, to change to a directory called mysite/webpages/, the command to use would be cd mysite/webpages. It is also possible to move up a directory by entering cd.. and return to the user's root directory simply by typing cd. Once you have navigated to the appropriate directory, the following commands will be useful:

chmod	(change mode) used to alter who can read, write or execute a file
cp	(copy) copies a file
dir	(directory) lists files in a directory
exit	terminates a Telnet session

ls	(list) lists files in directory; may be used instead of dir
mkdir	(make directory) creates a directory
mv	(move) moves a file
pwd	(print working directory) lists the current directory
rm	(remove) deletes a file
rmdir	(remove directory) removes a directory
tar	(tap archive) unpacks tar (zip) files

These are only a few of the essential commands that can be used with UNIX but should be enough for setting up files on a server. Most of them work with 'arguments' or 'switches', modifiers that extend their functions or make them more specific, indicated by a prefix hyphen. Thus to see the attributes of a file in a directory (useful if you wish to see which files will be hidden from general users, or which ones are read only), type ls -l. You can also use ls -a to print all files in a directory, including hidden ones.

Setting permissions

With files on the site, the final step may be to make them accessible to visitors to the site. UNIX can set permissions for who can access files down to the individual file level, which is important for security (for example, to hide certain files from general visitors but enable them to those with passwords). These permissions are set for the owner of the file (usually the person who created it), groups and other users.

Using ls -l provides a file list showing permissions, which is divided into four fields, - rwx rwx rwx, indicating the file type (usually a hyphen to represent a file, or d for a directory) and whether the owner, a specific group or other users can read (r), write to (w) or execute (x) a file: if one of these permissions is not granted, the letter is replaced by a hyphen. For example, d rwx r-x r-- indicates a directory in which the owner may read, write to and execute files as he or she wishes, a specific group may read and execute files from, and which all other users may only read.

Changing file permissions requires the chmod command, which can be used with either letters or numbers (using an octal system, from 0 to 7, where 0 provides no permissions and 7 provides all). For example, chmod +r myfile activates read permissions on myfile for all users. Two commonly used numbers are chmod 755 myfile, which activates read and execute status for a file but only allows the owner to write to it, and chmod 644 myfile, setting read permissions for everyone, but allowing no one to execute the file and reserving write to status for the owner.

Security

No computer is entirely safe. AT&T, for example, reports that on average its systems are attacked on the Internet once a day; smaller companies attract less attention, but with a server connected permanently to the Internet, security becomes a more important issue. When placing information on the Net, be proactive: find the most vulnerable spots in your system and determine the worst that could happen were it to be attacked. Data that is critical should be protected both internally and externally (and placing information on the Internet may alert you to security aspects you had not been concerned with before). As well as serious threats such as crackers and damage from viruses, anyone responsible for managing a web site should be aware of the threats from environmental dangers.

Cracking (the term for criminal hacking), like burglary, is a real threat on the Net, but it should not deter you from setting up a site. Most intruders, like most viruses, are relatively harmless if you are well protected and backed up. Attacks on web sites could, however, result in data being stolen or corrupted, or even simply system crashes. These are rare but still occur (41 per cent of companies with between ten and ninety-nine employees experienced an information breach according to a 1998 DTI report), and so it is important to be aware of the risks and adopt a strategy to prevent problems wherever possible. Obviously, the damaging effects of system failure or data loss are most evident when running a business, but other web producers may suffer if they do not plan ahead – a student producing work for assessment, for example.

Password protection is only the first key to Internet security, but it is an obvious one: using easily recognisable passwords provides one of the easiest means to bypass any security you may have in place, and the advice given in chapter one for creating a password is even more important for the web administrator than for the web user.

Two of the measures you can take to deter illegal entry are encryption and firewalls. Encryption uses two keys for every transaction: one key encrypts a file, making it unintelligible, the other decodes it. Key escrow, a method favoured by the UK and US governments but condemned by experts as less safe, places a public key in the hands of a third party which may be used by authorities to decode files. In contrast to encryption, a firewall works by sealing off a network from the Internet and only allows authorised traffic to enter; such a firewall must be regularly audited, however, as even one weak link on a network can open up other computers.

Viruses are worth a special mention as they are the most common security threat to using the Internet. Again, it is not worth letting fear of viruses deter you from using the Net – most viruses are relatively harmless if important data is backed up. There are occasional disasters, but these are very rare: most incidents involve the loss of only very small amounts of data, which can be a nuisance. When using the Internet, always ensure that you regularly run anti-virus software and download latest releases from the manufacturer's web site.

PROMOTING A SITE

First contact

One of the most common claims from just about any ISP attempting to sell web space and services is that one of the primary uses of the Internet is for marketing and branding a site. While this may mean that most users still have not worked out practical uses for the Net, it is also true that a web site can provide useful information about an individual, company or service in an increasingly wired world.

To be effective, a web site does not work in isolation: at the very least it should offer some form of contact for visitors who may require further or more specific information. In addition, an email update or posting to a relevant newsgroup will help draw attention to your web site. Emailing can be a sensitive topic. Web producers should never send out unsolicited email – spamming almost never succeeds and generates more bad customer responses than good ones. Used properly, however (and that means gaining permission before sending out emails), email can be a positive tool in conjunction with a web presence.

As well as using newsgroups and email there are other techniques for getting visitors to your site. For many users the main route into your site will be via links from other sites or, more commonly, from search engines. Setting up links may take several forms: if producers of sites of related interest are willing, you may be able to place reciprocal links in their web site in return for links from yours. Increasingly, banner advertisements are an acceptable means of communicating links (see 'Advertising on the web' below).

The first stage to ensuring that a web site appears in search engines is to register it with search engines. Such engines use 'spiders' to search the web, processing the contents of a page, but you can also speed up the process by visiting a search engine home page, and most have a link to submit information about your page. To take the effort out of this, consider using www.submit-it.com: there is a charge for this, but it speeds up registration with all major search engines rather than going through the process yourself or waiting for them to find you (if they do at all). The index page of a site should include keywords and description tags so that it can be searched for more easily (see 'Using Meta tags').

Rather than relying on your web site to sell itself simply by virtue of personal or business information, a good trick is to include information that is likely to be picked up by search engines and will appeal to a wider range of web surfers. For example, someone who wishes to promote their cart-racing track may keep an updated list of Formula 1 race statistics, or a music distributor could provide additional background data on different groups. The time spent creating an impartial guide to a relevant topic can pay dividends if it encourages people to return to your site and spend more time there.

TIPS FOR SITE PROMOTION

Marketing your site is an inexact science, but here are a few pointers:

- **Use your web address:** Your web address should appear everywhere your phone number appears.

- **Don't rely on the web alone:** Email can be a particularly useful tool to provide updates and reminders, as well as information targeted to requests.

- **Provide additional services:** Offer extra information around your core interest that will bring in extra visitors.

- **Keep emails you send out:** This is the best way to track information you send out and so avoid overloading visitors with irrelevant information.

- **Don't spam:** Do not use bulk email applications; most addresses included on these lists will be irrelevant and earn you a poor reputation. Ask for permission before you mail.

- **Register data:** If you collect information on visitors, you need to register your site to be compliant with the Data Protection Act.

- **Check the relevancy of newsgroups:** If you are promoting your web site on a newsgroup, ensure that the announcement is brief and relevant (read some sample postings beforehand) unless you wish to generate complaints.

Using Meta tags

While the important work in a web page seems to occur in between the <BODY> and </BODY> tags where images, text, links and other elements are displayed, the <HEAD> … </HEAD> tags also contain other important information which can be useful for your pages when hosted on a web server.

In addition to carrying the title of a page and scripts, the HEAD section contains information that is used by search engines when trawling through the Internet indexing various pages. The <TITLE> … </TITLE> tag itself is employed by some engines to provide relevant information, but more powerful tags are the <META> tags, document information tags that provide important data to browsers, servers and search engines.

The most often used META attributes are NAME and CONTENT, which are used together, for example:

```
<META NAME="Keywords" CONTENT="Kernow: Cornish
history and places">
```

Such a tag informs search engines that anyone interested in Cornwall should visit this site.

Though keywords are a primary use for Meta tags, these also perform other functions that are important to the maintenance of a site. First of all, <META HTTP-EQUIV="refresh" CONTENT="10"; URL = http://www.myserver.com/mysite.htm"> will redirect compatible browsers to a new site after ten seconds. When using such a tag, be sure to include something in the body of the page – including an alternative link – in case the browser does not work with this tag. In addition, the <META HTTP-EQUIV="expires" CONTENT= "Sat. 01 Jan 2000 00:00:00"> will force a **proxy server**, that is a server housing temporary copies of a site, to reload a page from its original source once the expiry date has been reached. Use of an expiry date set in the past means your page will never be cached, which is handy if it is updated regularly.

Advertising on the web

Banner advertisements, first introduced by *Hotwired*, have become ubiquitous on the web. Visitors clicking on these inch-high advertisements for anything from processors to Porsches are taken to the advertiser's pages for more information and, increasingly, the chance to buy online. Advertising on the web is of interest for two reasons for web producers: first, it is an opportunity to make money from a web site; second, it may serve as a means of promoting a site.

Payment for advertisements works in a number of ways, the most common being per page impression. Typical payments at the time of writing are £25 per thousand impressions, so an advertisement that is seen 100,000 times would cost £2,500, and some services allow users to specify a number and amount, the advertisement being withdrawn when that number is hit. Considering that page advertisements in magazines cost this much or less, this may not be such a good deal for the amount of space involved.

An alternative is click-through rates, where a much larger fee (around £150) is charged only for those visitors who click on the banner to be taken to your site. These prices, however, are taken from rate cards, and it may be possible to find discounts, particularly as web advertising in the UK has been slow to take off.

If you are using advertising to promote your site, there are a few issues that you should be aware of. First of all, even on a well-targeted web site, an advertisement is unlikely to achieve higher than a 10 per cent click-through rate; on a poorly targeted site, that figure will be closer to zero per cent. In effect, much advertising on the web, as with television or magazines, is impression advertising and brand marketing.

In addition, beware less-scrupulous web sites that use such things as a large number of frames to increase page impressions or extra navigation clicks to get to important information. ABC //electronic (www.abc. org.uk/electronic) is now tightening its web auditing, so that impression rates include a combination of files to produce one page.

Auditing site use

Of course, another feature of producing for the web may be that you are hosting advertisements rather than using them to promote your own site. If this is the case, you will probably need to audit advertising on your site to provide information for advertisers.

Most auditing software relies on information provided by a browser to track visits, but this may not be as accurate as it initially appears. IP addresses are usually allocated dynamically by ISPs, meaning that a visitor who logs on with the address 195.75.123.100 may be 195.75.123.101 the next day, indicating two separate visitors rather than one. Alternatively, a large corporation with a single fixed IP address leading to a firewall may be hiding hundreds of visitors as one. Cookies can be used to check whenever the browser returns to the site, but many users will disable these. Again, if a site is cached, either on the user's own computer or on a proxy server, there is no hope of tracking such use.

That said, auditing advertising remains important; each time a request is made to a server, if logging facilities have been set up by the web server it will generate an entry into a log file (a text file containing details of IP address, time, date, and so on) which ISPs generally make available to commercial customers. Software such as Hitlist Pro (www. accrue.com), Webtrends (www.webtrends.com) and Analog (www.adbil-ity.com) works by taking the log files generated by web-server software and feeding it through spreadsheets to chart site usage.

Guidelines for privacy

The Internet is a conduit for a vast amount of data collected from users actively (via such things as forms) and passively (through cookies to profile visitors). As with loyalty cards, such information can be valuable to web producers in its own right, but anyone responsible for managing a web site also has to pay due attention to legislation covering data protection and privacy.

The 1984 and 1998 Data Protection Acts (which implement wider European Union Data Protection Directives) attempt to provide users with a degree of protection regarding the collection and use of such personal data. While there is also international legislation, enforcement of data protection is always difficult with a medium such as the web, where a complaint by a user may be made against a supplier in another jurisdiction. The fact that web sites may also be cached or mirrored adds to the difficulties of regulation, but privacy is a significant factor in e-commerce. GeoCities, for example, saw its share price fall when it was accused of mishandling data provided by users.

An attempt to implement good practice is the inclusion of privacy statements, which are a response to legislation and examples of self-regulation. As well as demonstrating compliance with EU legislation, such statements are often promoted as a means of providing a competitive edge, and include details of what data is being collected, who is collecting it, how long it will be stored, and the rights a consumer has with regard to access and correction/deletion.

If you are intending to produce a web site for business purposes, a privacy statement can serve as a clear indication to visitors that you are committed to good practice. Obviously, drawing attention to consumer rights is also the clearest way of inviting criticism should a site not implement such practice, so a privacy statement should be implemented in practice as well as in theory. For help in constructing a statement, visit TRUST-e (www.truste.org) or the OECD (www.oecd.org/dsti/sti/it/secur/index.html), which provide useful tools.

CONCLUDING REMARKS

In the introduction to this book, I began by explaining that while there are many techniques and concepts that can be taught with relation to web production, this should not be at the expense of imagination and ideas. There are many sites that I use on a regular basis, either because, as in the case of Pointcast (www.pointcast.co.uk) or Amazon (www.amazon.co.uk) they provide information or services in a format that is more convenient for me to use across the Internet, or because, like *Hotwired* (www.hotwired.com) or Britannica Online (www.britannica.com), they indicate the potential for this new medium to entertain and inform.

Throughout this book, you have been guided through the essential principles of web production which, as I have repeated several times, consist not only of techniques for placing text, images, links and interactive components on a page but also planning what the purpose of such a site should be. If nothing else, the preparation that goes into a web site should take into account what you wish to gain from it: web production can be an interesting and pleasurable pastime if nothing else.

At the same time, this book has concentrated on several fairly technical aspects of web design. If you choose to use a package such as Dreamweaver or GoLive, it is possible to build very competent and proficient sites without actually understanding what JavaScript is and how it works. And yet, as has been indicated several times, some understanding goes a long way, and those readers who cannot afford the latest and greatest programs can still build professional-looking sites with no more than a text editor and modem connection. Many areas of web design have often been hailed as a black art, but the growth of an Internet community and the availability of help and support on the web itself means that this medium has the potential to be more democratic than any other. With the right skills and imagination, the gateway to web world-wide production is open to more people than ever before.

Glossary

ActiveX A set of instructions devised by Microsoft that describes how objects interact with the browser and operating system (in contrast to Java, which only interacts with the browser).

ADSL Asymmetric Digital Subscriber Line. Offers a much faster link than analog modems across standard copper lines.

Apache The most popular web server software, originally developed for UNIX but available on other platforms.

applet A program designed to be launched from within another program, typically a browser.

ARPANET The network set up by the Advanced Research Projects Agency (ARPA) and the precursor to the Internet.

ASP Active Server Pages. Microsoft's scripting language for creating dynamic websites. Also used to refer to an Applications Service Provider, a company that offers software for hire across the web.

bandwidth The amount of information that can be transferred across an Internet connection.

bitmap A photographic image.

cache A temporary store of information downloaded from the Internet. Browsers look in the cache to speed up the process of downloading information.

CGI Common Gateway Interface. A protocol enabling web pages to transfer instructions to a server.

client-server A means of connecting computers whereby the server provides information that is accessed via the remote machine.

cookie A text message sent from a web server to a browser and then returned by the browser to the server when the user revisits that site. Cookies are generally used to identify users and store information between visits or generate statistics.

CSS   Cascading Style Sheets. Enable designers to specify the appearance of a page with two specifications: CSS1 for text formatting and CSS2 for text positioning.

DHTML   Or Dynamic HTML. The next generation of HTML, which incorporates cascading style sheets and scripting to offer more control over layout and greater interactivity.

DNS   Domain Name Services. The process by which IP addresses for registered domains are transformed into URL names (such as www.yahoo.com) and vice versa.

domain name   An address or URL for one or more web servers.

error correction protocol   A technique used by modems to cancel noise generated on lines and repeat transmissions if an error is made.

FAQ   Frequently Asked Question(s). A document designed to answer common queries and help new users.

firewall   Hardware or software designed to prevent unauthorised access to a network, which scrutinises all information entering or leaving the network and rejects it if it fails certain security criteria, such as coming from an unspecified address.

FTP   File Transfer Protocol. One of the main systems of rules governing the transfer of information across the Internet but also used to refer to a tool for accessing Internet data.

GIF   Graphic Interchange Format. An image format that uses 'lossless' compression to make files shorter so that no information is discarded. Can only support up to 256 colours, but can also be used with transparencies or animations.

HTML   Hypertext Markup Language. The series of formatting commands interpreted by the browser which determines how a page is displayed on the web.

HTTP   Hypertext Transfer Protocol. The communications protocol used to define how files link to each other and how information is transmitted to browsers.

hypertext   The presentation of documents that connect to other files or parts of the same document. Hypermedia is another term for such documents which also make use of images and multimedia elements to create links.

IAB   Internet Architecture Board. A non-governmental organisation responsible for governing protocols for communicating across the Internet.

ICANN   The Internet Corporation for Assigned Names and Numbers. Handles domain name registration and IP address allocation.

IETF   The Internet Engineering Task Force. Like the IAB, an organisation for establishing Internet standards, particularly responsible for the system of Requests for Comments (RFC).

IIS   Internet Information Server. Microsoft's web server included with Windows NT.

Internet   Typically defined as a 'network of networks', the Internet is a self-governing system that connects many thousands of servers and millions of users world wide. Computers join the Internet by subscribing to a series of standards (protocols) that define the range of services available to users.

intranet   An internal network of computers using the same software and protocols as the Internet and which may connect to the Internet.

IP   Internet Protocol. A series of numbers between 0 and 255 that create a unique address for each computer connected to the Internet.

IRC   Internet Relay Chat. A system of real-time based communication whereby users can send messages to others currently online.

ISDN   Integrated Services Digital Network. A means of transmitting digital information across phone lines which tends to be more reliable than analog modems.

ISOC   The Internet Society. One of the most important Internet regulatory bodies.

ISP   Internet Service Provider. An intermediary between the Internet and the end-user, an ISP can provide IP addresses and other services to subscribers.

Java   An object-oriented programming language that has the advantage of running across multiple operating systems by using a 'virtual machine' to interpret the original code on a particular platform.

JavaScript   A scripting language, originally called LiveScript, developed by Netscape and Sun to add interactivity to web pages.

JPEG   Joint Photographic Experts Group. A means of compressing images that is 'lossy', that is, extraneous information is discarded.

LAN   Local Area Network. A network of computers in a relatively small area such as an office or building, in contrast to a WAN, or wide area network, such as bank networks or the Internet.

Linux   Free version of UNIX incorporating software designed to run on the UNIX clone GNU (which stands for 'GNU's Not UNIX').

MIME   Multipurpose Internet Mail Extensions. A series of instructions enabling a browser to interpret different types of information.

modem   MOdulator/DEModulator. Connects a computer to the Internet across normal phone lines by translating digital signals into analog ones so they can be transmitted across copper wires, and vice versa so that they will be understood as information by the computer.

MP3 or MPEG3   A highly compressed format for sound which delivers near CD-quality audio.

MPEG   Motion Pictures Expert Group. A standard of video compression commonly used on the web.

node   A network terminal, or the point where the computer is connected to the network.

NSF   National Science Foundation. A US organisation previously responsible for administering the Internet.

packet   A unit of data sent as part of a file. Files are broken down into smaller chunks that can be sent to an address by several routes and reassembled at their destination.

PDF   Portable Document Format. A proprietary file format developed by Adobe to distribute documents with original formatting and widely used on the Internet.

Perl   Practical Extraction and Reporting Language. A scripting language that is commonly used on the Web to provide interactive and dynamic sites.

plug-in   Software used to extend the capabilities of a browser.

PNG   Portable Network Graphics. A new graphics format combining the best elements of GIF and JPEG images.

POP3   Post Office Protocol. A series of instructions governing incoming email.

port   The input for a specific Internet service, such as web, FTP or Telnet. Port numbers are used by software to connect to that service.

PPP   *See* SLIP

protocol   A rule or set of rules governing how computers and applications connect and communicate with each other.

proxy server   A server sitting between the user and the Internet that monitors all requests to check whether information is already stored on a local cache.

PWS   Personal Web Server. Developed by Microsoft for use on Windows platforms.

RFC   Request for Comments. The first stage in establishing a standard for Internet communications. RFCs are circulated to the Internet Engineering Task Force (IETF).

router   Examines packets of information and sends them on to their appropriate destination.

script   A means of extending the interactive capabilities of HTML via a series of instructions that are processed by a browser or application on the server.

server   A computer hosting documents and applications that can be accessed remotely by other computers.

SGML   Standard Generalised Markup Language. A set of formatting instructions from which HTML was developed.

Shockwave/Flash   Two proprietary formats for multimedia used by Macromedia and commonly encountered on the web.

SLIP/PPP   Serial Line Interface Protocol/Point to Point Protocol. Standards for connecting directly to the Internet from a client machine.

SMTP   Simple Mail Transfer Protocol. A series of rules governing the transmission of outgoing mail.

spam   Junk or other unsolicited email.

TCP   Transfer Control Protocol. Along with IP, this is the standard governing communication between all computers on the Internet.

Telnet   A protocol allowing users to log into a remote computer and use it as their own.

UNIX   Operating system developed by AT&T in the 1970s and the backbone of Internet operating systems.

URL   Uniform Resource Locator. The address of a page on the web.

Usenet   Newsgroup archives which are now incorporated into Internet services but which were originally text-only systems of bulletin boards running alongside the early Net.

vector   Used to refer to computer-generated drawings (a vector being a line between two points in a certain direction).

W3C   The World Wide Web Consortium. One of the non-governmental organisations responsible for governing standards for the web.

WAN   Wide Area Network. A network that is distributed over a large geographical area, the Internet being the most important.

web server   A computer that distributes, or serves, web pages to client computers.

XML   eXtensible Markup Language. A means of making web documents self-describing so that they can be formatted with database-style fields.

XSL   eXtensible Style Language. A means of defining styles for elements on a web page that can be changed via instructions from a browser.

HTML quick reference

The following is a compact reference to HTML tags. It is not complete, and concentrates on HTML 3.2 elements. For a more complete reference see the *Producing for the Web* site at www.producing.routledge.com/techniques.htm.

Each tag is followed by a description, as well as any attributes that may be included within the tag (for example the <FONT> mark-up may include <FONT SIZE=+1 COLOR="red">); these attributes are followed by an equals sign and an attribute. Empty tags are not followed by an end marker (such as <IMG>), while container tags are indicated by ellipsis (for example <BODY> ... </BODY>).

Tag	Description	Additional attributes
<A> ... </A>	Anchor marking a link	HREF=(URL)\NAME=(name)\ TARGET=(name)
<AREA>	Defines an area of an image map	COORDS=(x, y, x, y)\ HREF=(URL)\NOHREF\SHAPE=(rect, rectangle, circ, circle, poly, polygon)\TARGET=(name)
<B> ... </B>	Bold style text	
<BLOCKQUOTE> ... <BLOCKQUOTE>	Indents text as a quote	
<BODY> ... <BODY>	The main content of an HTML document	ALINK=(colour)\BACKGROUND= (URL)\BGCOLOR=(background colour)\LINK=(colour)\TEXT=(colour) \VLINK=(colour)
 	Line break	
<CAPTION> ... </CAPTION>	Applies a caption to a table	ALIGN=(top, bottom)
<CENTER> ... </CENTER>	Centres page content	
<DD> ... </DD>	Definition description	
<DIR> ... </DIR>	Directory list, containing list items <LI>	
<DL> ... </DL>	Definition list used for dictionary items with <DT> and <DD>	
<DT> ... </DT>	Definition term	
<EM> ... </EM>	Emphasis	
<FONT> ... </FONT>	Font attributes	SIZE=(+ or − number)\ COLOR=(colour)
<FORM> ... </FORM>	Defines a form for user input	ACTON=(URL)\METHOD=(GET, POST)
<FRAME> ... </FRAME>	Frame definition	FRAMEBORDER=(yes, no)\ MARGINHEIGHT=\(number of pixels) \MARGINWIDTH=\(number of pixels)\NAME=(name, _blank, _self, _parent, _top)\ NORESIZE\SCROLLING=(yes, no, auto)\SRC=URL
<FRAMESET> ... </FRAMESET>	Main divisions for frames on a page	ROWS=(pixels, percent, number of characters)\COLS=(pixels, percent, number of characters)
<H1> ... </H1>	Level 1 heading; replace 1 with a number from 2–6 for headings for levels 2–6	
<HEAD> ... </HEAD>	The head of a document containing information about that document	
<HR>	Horizontal rule (line) across the page	SIZE=(number of pixels)\ WIDTH=(percent of page)\ NOSHADE
<HTML> ... </HTML>	Defines the beginning and end of an HTML document	
<I> ... </I>	Italics	

Tag	Description	Additional attributes
<IMG>	Places inline image on page	SRC=(URL)\ALT=(alternative text)\ALIGN=(left, right, top, middle, bottom, texttop, absmiddle, baseline, absbottom)\BORDER=(number of pixels)\HEIGHT=(number of pixels)\HSPACE=(number of pixels)\VSPACE=(number of pixels)\WIDTH=(number of pixels)
<INPUT>	Defines input objects on forms	ALIGN=(left, right, top, middle bottom, texttop, absmiddle, baseline, absbottom)\CHECKED\HEIGHT= (number of pixels)\ MAXLENGTH=(number of characters)\NAME=(name)\SIZE= (number of characters)\ SRC=(URL)\TUPE=(TEXT, CHECKBOX, RADIO, SUBMIT, RESENT, HIDDEN, IMAGE)\VALUE=(text)\WIDTH= (number of pixels)
<LI> ... </LI>	List item	
<MAP> ... </MAP>	Client-side image map	NAME=(name)
<MENU> ... </MENU>	Menu list using <LI>	
<NOFRAMES> ... </NOFRAMES>	Displays alternative content for browsers that cannot support frames	
<OL> ... </OL>	Ordered list using <LI>	START=(number)\Type=(name)
<P> ... </P>	Paragraph break	
<PRE> ... </PRE>	Pre-formatted text	
<SMALL> ... </SMALL>	Smaller font for text	
<STRONG> ... </STRONG>	Strong emphasis	
_{...}	Subscript	
^{...}	Superscript	
<TABLE> ... </TABLE>	Defines a table	ALIGN=(left, right)\ BGCOLOR=(background colour)\ BORDER=(number of pixels)\CELLPADDING=\(number of pixels)\CELLSPACING=(number of pixels)\RULES=(none, basic, rows)
<TD> ... </TD>	Table data cell	ALIGN=(left, center, right)\ COLSPAN=(number)\ ROWSPAN=(number)\VALIGN=(top, middle, bottom)
<TH> ... </TH>	Table header cell with bold, centred contents	ALIGN=(left, center, right)\ COLSPAN=(number)\ ROWSPAN=(number)\VALIGN=(top, middle, bottom)
<TITLE> ... </TITLE>	Document title, included in document head	ALIGN=(left, center, right)\ VALIGN=(top, middle, bottom)
<TR> ... </TR>	Table row	
<U> ... </U>	Underline	
<UL> ... </UL>	Unordered list using <LI>	TYPE=(circle, disc, square)

Resources

The following is a list of books and web sites that may be useful for further reading and for help when building web components. For a more complete list of annotated resources, updated on a regular basis with links to new web resources, see the *Producing for the Web* site at www.producing.routledge.com/resources.htm.

INTERNET HISTORY AND BACKGROUND

Berners-Lee, Tim, *Weaving the Web*, Orion, 1999
Cooper, Jonathan (ed.) *Liberating Cyberspace: Civil Liberties, Human Rights and the Internet*, Pluto Press, 1999
Jonscher, Charles, *Wired Life: Who Are We in the Digital Age?*, Bantam Press, 1999
Naughton, John, *A Brief History of the Future: The Origins of the Internet*, Weidenfeld and Nicholson, 1999
Reid, Robert H., *Architects of the Web*, John Wiley, 1997
Seigel, David, *Futurize your Enterprise: Business Strategy in the Age of the E-Consumer*, John Wiley, 1999

www.ietf.org	the Internet Engineering Task Force, responsible for Internet standards
www.isoc.org	the Internet Society, which promotes Internet development
www.w3c.org	the World Wide Web Consortium, responsible for technical standards across the web

WEB DESIGN AND HTML

Carlson, Jeff, and Fleischman, Glenn, *Real World Adobe GoLive 4*, Peachpit Press, 1999
Fleming, Jennifer, *Web Navigation: Designing the User Experience*, O'Reilly, 1998
Gutzman, Alexis, and Pfaffenberger, Bryan, *HTML 4 Bible*, IDG Books, 1998
Karpinski, Richard, *Beyond HTML*, Osborne McGraw-Hill, 1996

Ladd, Eric, and O'Donnell, Jim, *Platinum Edition Using HTML 4, XML and Java 1.2*, Macmillan, 1998

Lopuck, Lisa, and Hampton, Sheryl, *Adobe Seminars: Web Page Design*, Adobe Press, 1997

Lowery, Joseph W., *Dreamweaver 2 Bible*, IDG Books, 1999

Musciano, Chuck, and Kennedy, Bill, *HTML: The Definitive Guide*, O'Reilly, 1998

Niederst, Jennifer, *Web Design in a Nutshell*, O'Reilly, 1998

Sather, Andrew, Ibanez, Ardith, and Dechant, Bernie, *Creating Killer Interactive Web Sites: The Art of Integrating Interactivity and Design*, Hayden Books, 1997

Siegel, David, *Creating Killer Web Sites*, Hayden Books, 2nd edition, 1997

Spainhour, Steven, and Eckstein, Robert, *Webmaster in a Nutshell*, O'Reilly, 1999

Towers, J. Tarin, *Dreamweaver 2*, Peachpit Press, 1999

Veen, Jeffrey, *Hotwired Style: Principles for Building Smart Web Sites*, Hardwired, 1997

Weinman, Lynda, and Pirouz, Raymond, *Click Here: Web Communication Design*, New Riders, 1997

hotwired.lycos.com/ webmonkey/	a good web developer's resource from *Wired* magazine
www.bensplanet.com	a complete HTML reference guide
www.nic.uk	registration service for UK domain names
www.skill.org.uk	the national bureau for students with disabilities; includes guidelines for web development
www.submit-it.com	automates the submitting of URLs to search engines
www.tucows.com	a large resource of tools and software
www.unplug.com/great/	design tips and resources for web developers
www.webtrends.com	software for managing and auditing web sites

GRAPHICS AND MULTIMEDIA

Cohen, Luanne, *Design Essentials*, Adobe Press, 1999

Cohen, Sandee, *Fireworks 2 for Windows and Macintosh*, Peachpit Press, 1999

Eigen, Brad J., and Livingston, Dan, *Essential Photoshop 5 for Web Professionals*, Prentice Hall, 1999

Fries, Martin, and Fries, Bruce, *The MP3 and Internet Audio Handbook*, Teamcom, 1999

Hamlin, J. Scott, *Effective Web Animation*, Addison-Wesley, 1999

Kyle, Lynn, *Essential Flash 4 for Web Professionals*, Prentice Hall, 1999

Lowery, Joseph W., and Griffin, Dennis, *Fireworks 2 Bible*, IDG Books, 1999

Patterson, Jeff, and Melcher, Ryan, *Audio on the Web: The Official IUMA Guide*, 1998

Persidsky, Andre, *Director 7 for Macintosh and Windows*, Peachpit Press, 1999

Ulrich, Katherine, *Flash 4 for Windows and Macintosh*, Peachpit Press, 1999

Wagstaff, Sean, and Collins, Corbin, *Animation on the Web*, Peachpit Press, 1998

Webster, Timothy, Atzberger, Paul, and Zolli, Andrew, *Web Designer's Guide To Graphics: PNT, GIF and JPEG*, Hayden Books, 1997

Weinman, Lynda, and Lentz, Jon, *Deconstructing Web Graphics 2*, New Riders, 1998
Willmore, Ben, *Adobe Photoshop 5 Studio Techniques*, Adobe Press, 1999

3bgraphics.hypermart.net	useful source of buttons, bars and backgrounds (hence the 3 'B's)
ftp://ftp.sunet.se/pub/ pictures/	large collection of public domain images
www.4yeo.org	colour-coordinated selections of a wide range of icons and images
www.abcgiant.com	another large collection of images
www.boutell.com/mapedit	useful for creating image maps
www.coolarchive.com	icons, images and audio resources arranged by type
www.macromedia.com	the premier site for multimedia tools across the web
www.real.com	contains useful tools for using and producing streaming media
www.webclipart.com	free clipart and tips on using images on the web

CGI AND DYNAMIC HTML

Barrett, Dan, Livingstone, Dan, and Brown, Micah, *Essential JavaScript for Web Professionals*, Prentice Hall, 1999
Busczek, Greg, *Instant ASP Scripts*, McGraw-Hill, 1999
Dwight, Jeffrey, Erwin, Michael, and Niles, Robert, *Special Edition Using CGI*, Que, 1997
Francis, Brian, Ullman, Chris, Sussman, David, *et al.*, *Beginning Active Server Pages 2.0*, Wrox, 1998
Goodman, Danny, *Dynamic HTML: The Definitive Reference*, O'Reilly, 1998
Goodman, Danny, and Eich, Brendan, *JavaScript Bible*, IDG, 1998
Heinle, Nick, and Siegel, David, *Designing with JavaScript: Creating Dynamic Web Pages*, O'Reilly, 1997
Isaacs, Scott, *Inside Dynamic HTML*, Microsoft Press, 1997
Ivler, J. M., and Husain, Kamran, *CGI Developer's Resource: Web Programming in TCL and Perl*, Prentice Hall, 1997
Lie, Hakon, Bos, Bert, and Cailliau, Robert, *Cascading Style Sheets, Second Edition: Designing for the Web*, Addison-Wesley, 1999
Livingston, Dan, and Brown, Micah, *Essential CSS and DHTML for Web Professionals*, Prentice Hall, 1999
McFarlaine, Nigel, *Instant JavaScript*, Wrox Press, 1997
Mudry, Robert, *The DHTML Companion*, Prentice Hall, 1998
Schwartz, Randal, and Christiansen, Tom, *Learning Perl/TK*, O'Reilly, 1997
Wall, Larry, Christiansen, Tom, and Schwartz, Randal L., *Programming Perl*, O'Reilly, 2nd edition, 1996
Wyke, R. Allen, and Ting, Charlton, *Pure JavaScript*, Sams, 1999

www.apache.org	the home site of the popular web server, Apache
www.bcentral.com	a large collection of CGI scripts and services
www.beseen.com	includes search engines, hit counters and navigation tools
www.cgi101.com	another collection of CGI scripts
www.freefind.com	a free search engine for your site
www.perl.org	the home site of this powerful scripting tool
www.responders.net	third-party form processing
www.ufbs.co.uk	a collection of Perl and CGI scripts
www.worldwidemart.com	another collection of CGI and Perl scripts
www.websiteresources.net	Microsoft's web development site

JAVA AND ACTIVEX

Armstrong, Tom, Crespino, Jim, and Alumbaugh, Rob, *Active Xpert*, Mc-Graw Hill, 1997
Flanagan, David, *Java in a Nutshell*, O'Reilly, 3rd edition, 1999
Lang, Zane, *ActiveX All in One: A Web Developer's Guide*, Prentice Hall, 1997
Walsh, Aaron E., and Fronckowiak, John, *Java Bible*, IDG Books, 1998

javaboutique.internet.com/	Java applets, articles and discussion groups
java.sun.com/applets/index.html	Sun's home site for free Java applets
www.activex.org	home site of the ActiveX working group
www.active-x.com	a large collection of ActiveX tools and utilities
www.developer.com/downloads	graphics, scripts and dynamic behaviours to add to your site
www.devpower.com	ActiveX tools for web developers
www.gamelan.com/	a wide range of Java applets are stored here
www.javasoft.com/applets/	information on Java and reusable examples

WRITING

Aitchinson, James, *Guide to Written English*, Cassell, 1996
Bagnall, Nicholas, *Newspaper Language*, Butterworth/Heinemann, 1993
Burchfield, Robert, *The New Fowler's Modern English Usage*, Clarendon, 1996
Greenbaum, Sidney, and Whitcut, Janet, *Longman Guide to English Usage*, Penguin, 1996
Hicks, Wynford, with Adams, Sally, and Gilbert, Harriett, *Writing for Journalists*, Routledge, 2nd edition, 1999
Hoffman, Ann, *Research for Writers*, A & C Black, 1992
Partridge, Eric, *Usage and Abusage*, Penguin, 1973
The Oxford Dictionary for Writers and Editors, Oxford University Press, 1981

Index